Letters on the English; or Lettres Philosophiques

Voltaire

Letters on the English; or Lettres Philosophiques

Table of Contents

Letters on the English; or Lettres Philosophiques 1
    Voltaire 1
    Letter I: On The Quakers 2
    Letter II: On The Quakers 6
    Letter III: On The Quakers 8
    Letter IV: On The Quakers 11
    Letter V: On The Church Of England 14
    Letter VI: On The Presbyterians 17
    Letter VII: On The Socinians, Or Arians, Or Antitrinitarians 18
    Letter VIII: On The Parliament 20
    Letter IX: On The Government 22
    Letter X: On Trade 26
    Letter XI: On Inoculation 27
    Letter XII: On The Lord Bacon 31
    Letter XIII: On Mr. Locke 35
    Letter XIV: On Descartes And Sir Isaac Newton 40
    Letter XV: On Attraction 45
    Letter XVI: On Sir Isaac Newton's Optics 53
    Letter XVII: On Infinites In Geometry, And Sir Isaac Newton's Chronology 56
    Letter XVIII: On Tragedy 61
    Letter XIX: On Comedy 65
    Letter XX: On Such Of The Nobility As Cultivate The Belles Lettres 69
    Letter XXI: On The Earl Of Rochester And Mr. Waller 71
    Letter XXII: On Mr. Pope And Some Other Famous Poets 75
    Letter XXIII: On The Regard That Ought To Be Shown To Men Of Letters 79
    Letter XXIV: On The Royal Society And Other Academies 82

Letters on the English; or Lettres Philosophiques

Voltaire

Kessinger Publishing reprints thousands of hard-to-find books!

Visit us at http://www.kessinger.net

- Letter I: On The Quakers
- Letter II: On The Quakers
- Letter III: On The Quakers
- Letter IV: On The Quakers
- Letter V: On The Church Of England
- Letter VI: On The Presbyterians
- Letter VII: On The Socinians, Or Arians, Or Antitrinitarians
- Letter VIII: On The Parliament
- Letter IX: On The Government
- Letter X: On Trade
- Letter XI: On Inoculation
- Letter XII: On The Lord Bacon
- Letter XIII: On Mr. Locke
- Letter XIV: On Descartes And Sir Isaac Newton
- Letter XV: On Attraction
- Letter XVI: On Sir Isaac Newton's Optics
- Letter XVII: On Infinites In Geometry, And Sir Isaac Newton's Chronology
- Letter XVIII: On Tragedy
- Letter XIX: On Comedy
- Letter XX: On Such Of The Nobility As Cultivate The Belles Lettres
- Letter XXI: On The Earl Of Rochester And Mr. Waller
- Letter XXII: On Mr. Pope And Some Other Famous Poets
- Letter XXIII: On The Regard That Ought To Be Shown To Men Of Letters
- Letter XXIV: On The Royal Society And Other Academies

Letters on the English; or Lettres Philosophiques

Letter I: On The Quakers

I was of opinion that the doctrine and history of so extraordinary a people were worthy the attention of the curious. To acquaint myself with them I made a visit to one of the most eminent Quakers in England, who, after having traded thirty years, had the wisdom to prescribe limits to his fortune and to his desires, and was settled in a little solitude not far from London. Being come into it, I perceived a small but regularly built house, vastly neat, but without the least pomp of furniture. The Quaker who owned it was a hale, ruddy complexioned old man, who had never been afflicted with sickness because he had always been insensible to passions, and a perfect stranger to intemperance. I never in my life saw a more noble or a more engaging aspect than his. He was dressed like those of his persuasion, in a plain coat without pleats in the sides, or buttons on the pockets and sleeves; and had on a beaver, the brims of which were horizontal like those of our clergy. He did not uncover himself when I appeared, and advanced towards me without once stooping his body; but there appeared more politeness in the open, humane air of his countenance, than in the custom of drawing one leg behind the other, and taking that from the head which is made to cover it. "Friend," says he to me, "I perceive thou art a stranger, but if I can do any thing for thee, only tell me." "Sir," said I to him, bending forwards and advancing, as is usual with us, one leg towards him, "I flatter myself that my just curiosity will not give you the least offense, and that you'll do me the honour to inform me of the particulars of your religion." "The people of thy country," replied the Quaker, "are too full of their bows and compliments, but I never yet met with one of them who had so much curiosity as thy self. Come in, and let us first dine together." I still continued to make some very unreasonable ceremonies, it not being easy to disengage one's self at once from habits we have been long used to; and after taking part in a frugal meal, which began and ended with a prayer to God, I began to question my courteous host. I opened with that which good Catholics have more than once made to Huguenots. "My

Letters on the English; or Lettres Philosophiques

dear sir," said I, "were you ever baptized?" "I never was," replied the Quaker, "nor any of my brethren." "Zounds!" said I to him, "you are not Christians, then." "Friend," replies the old man in a soft tone of voice, "swear not; we are Christians, and endeavour to be good Christians, but we are not of opinion that the sprinkling water on a child's head makes him a Christian." "Heavens!" said I, shocked at his impiety, "you have then forgot that Christ was baptised by St. John." "Friend," replies the mild Quaker once again, "swear not; Christ indeed was baptised by John, by He himself never baptised anyone. We are the disciples of Christ, not of John." I pitied very much the sincerity of my worthy Quaker, and was absolutely for forcing him to get himself christened. "Were that all," replied he very gravely, "we would submit cheerfully to baptism, purely in compliance with thy weakness, for we don't condemn any person who uses it; but then we think that those who profess a religion of so holy, so spiritual a nature as that of Christ, ought to abstain to the utmost of their power from the Jewish ceremonies." "O unaccountable!" said I: "what! baptism a Jewish ceremony?" "Yes, my friend," says he, "so truly Jewish, that a great many Jews use the baptism of John to this day. Look into ancient authors, and thou wilt find that John only revived this practice; and that it had been used by the Hebrews, long before his time, in like manner as the Mahometans imitated the Ishmaelites in their pilgrimages to Mecca. Jesus indeed submitted to the baptism of John, as He had suffered Himself to be circumcised; but circumcision and the washing with water ought to be abolished by the baptism of Christ, that baptism of the Spirit, that ablution of the soul, which is the salvation of mankind. Thus the forerunner said, 'I indeed baptise you with water unto repentance; but He that cometh after me is mightier that I, whose shoes I am not worthy to bear: He shall baptise you with the Holy Ghost and with fire.' Likewise Paul, the great apostle of the Gentiles, writes as follows to the Corinthians, 'Christ sent me not to baptise, but to preach the Gospel;' and indeed Paul never baptised but two persons with water, and that very much against his inclinations. He circumcised his disciple Timothy, and the other disciples likewise all who were willing to submit to that carnal ordinance. "But art thou circumcised?" added he. "I have not the honour to be so," said I. "Well, friend," continued the Quaker, "thou art a Christian without being circumcised, and I am one without being baptised." Thus did this pious man make a wrong, but very specious application of four or five texts of Scripture which seemed to favour the tenets of his sect; but at the same time forgot very sincerely a hundred texts which made directly against them. I had more sense than to contest with him, since there is no possibility of convincing an enthusiast. A man should never pretend to inform a lover of his mistress' faults, no more than one who is at law of the badness of his cause; nor attempt to win over a fanatic by strength of reasoning. Accordingly I waived the subject.

"Well", said I to him, "what sort of a communion have you?" "We have none like that thou hintest at among us," replied he. "How! no communion?" said I. "Only that spiritual one," replied he, "of hearts." He then began again to throw out his texts of Scripture; and preached a most eloquent sermon against that ordinance. He harangued in a tone as though he had been inspired, to prove that the sacraments were merely of human invention, and that the word "sacrament" was not once mentioned in the Gospel. "Excuse," said he, "my ignorance, for I have not employed a hundredth part of the arguments which might be brought to prove the truth of our religion, but these thou thyself mayest peruse in the Exposition of our Faith written by Robert Barclay. It is one of the best pieces that ever was penned by man; and as our adversaries confess it to be of dangerous tendency, the arguments in it must necessarily be very convincing." I promised to peruse this piece, and my Quaker imagined he had already made a convert of me. He afterwards gave me an account in few words of some singularities which make this sect the contempt of others. "Confess," said he, "that it was very difficult for thee to refrain from laughter, when I answered all thy civilities without uncovering my head, and at the same time said 'thee' and 'thou' to thee. However, thou appearest to me too well read not to know that in Christ's time no nation was so ridiculous as to put the plural number for the singular. Augustus Caesar himself was spoken to in such phrases as these: 'I love thee,' 'I beseech thee,' 'I thank thee;' but he did not allow any person to call him 'Domine,' sir. It was not till many ages after that men would have the word 'you,' as though they were double, instead of 'thou' employed in speaking to them; and usurped the flattering titles of lordship, of eminence, and of holiness, which mere worms bestow on other worms by assuring them that they are with a most profound respect, and an infamous falsehood, their most obedient humble servants. It is to secure ourselves more strongly from such a shameless traffic of lies and flattery, that we 'thee' and 'thou' a king with the same freedom as we do a beggar, and salute no person; we owing nothing to mankind but charity, and to the laws respect and obedience.

"Our apparel is also somewhat different from that of others, and this purely, that it may be a perpetual warning to us not to imitate them. Others wear the badges and marks of their several dignities, and we those of Christian humility. We fly from all assemblies of pleasure, from diversions of every kind, and from places where gaming is practised; and, indeed, our case would be very deplorable, should we fill with such levities as those I have mentioned the heart which ought to be the habitation of God. We never swear, not even in a court of justice, being of opinion that the most holy name of God ought not to be prostituted in the miserable contests betwixt man and man. When we are obliged to appear before a magistrate upon other people's account (for lawsuits are unknown among the Friends), we give evidence to the truth by sealing it with our yea or nay; and the judges believe us on our bare affirmation, whilst so many other Christians forswear themselves on the holy Gospels. We never war or fight in any case; but it is not that we are afraid, for so far from shuddering at the thoughts of death, we on the contrary bless the moment which unites us with the Being of Beings; but the reason of our not using the outward sword is, that we are neither wolves, tigers, nor mastiffs, but men and Christians. Our God, who has commanded us to love our enemies, and to suffer without repining, would certainly not permit us to cross the seas, merely because murderers clothed in scarlet, and wearing caps two foot high, enlist citizens by a noise made with two little sticks on an ass' skin extended. And when, after a victory is gained, the whole city of London is illuminated; when the sky is in a blaze with fireworks, and a noise is heard in the air, of thanksgivings, of bells, of organs, and of the cannon, we groan in silence, and are deeply affected with sadness of spirit and brokenness of heart, for the sad havoc which is the occasion of those

Letters on the English; or Lettres Philosophiques

public rejoicings."

Letter II: On The Quakers

Such was the substance of the conversation I had with this very singular person; but I was greatly surprised to see him come the Sunday following and take me with him to the Quakers' meeting. There are several of these in London, but that which he carried me to stands near the famous pillar called The Monument. The brethren were already assembled at my entering it with my guide. There might be about four hundred men and three hundred women in the meeting. The women hid their faces behind their fans, and the men were covered with their broad-brimmed hats. All were seated, and the silence was universal. I passed through them, but did not perceive so much as one lift up his eyes to look at me. This silence lasted a quarter of an hour, when at last one of them rose up, took off his hat, and, after making a variety of wry faces and groaning in a most lamentable manner, he, partly from his nose and partly from his mouth, threw out a strange, confused jumble of words (borrowed, as he imagined, from the Gospel) which neither himself nor any of his hearers understood. When this distorter had ended his beautiful soliloquy, and that the stupid, but greatly edified, congregation were separated, I asked my friend how it was possible for the judicious part of their assembly to suffer such a babbling? "We are obliged," said he, "to suffer it, because no one knows when a man rises up to hold forth whether he will be moved by the Spirit or by folly. In this doubt and uncertainty we listen patiently to everyone; we even allow our women to hold forth. Two or three of these are often inspired at one and the same time, and it is then that a most charming noise is heard in the Lord's house." "You have, then, no priests?" said I to him. "No, no, friend," rfplies the Quaker, "to our great happiness." Then opening one of the Friends' books, as he called it, he read the following words in an emphatic tone:–"'God forbid we should presume to ordain anyone to receive the Holy Spirit on the Lord's Day to the prejudice of the rest of the brethren.' Thanks to the Almighty, we are the only people upon earth that have no priests. Wouldst thou deprive us of so happy a distinction? Why should we abandon our babe to mercenary nurses, when we ourselves have milk enough for it? These mercenary creatures would soon domineer in our houses and destroy both the mother and the babe. God has said, 'Freely you have received, freely give.' Shall we, after these words, cheapen, as it were, the Gospel, sell the Holy Ghost, and make of an assembly of Christians a mere shop of traders? We don't pay a set of men clothed in black to assist our poor, to bury our dead, or to preach to the brethren. These offices are all of too tender a nature for us ever to entrust them to others." "But how it is possible for you," said I, with some warmth, "to know whether your discourse is really inspired by the Almighty?" "Whosoever," says he, "shall implore Christ to enlighten him, and shall publish the Gospel truths, he may feel inwardly, such a one may be assured that he is inspired by the Lord." He then poured forth a numberless multitude of Scripture texts which proved, as he imagined, that there is no such thing as Christianity without an immediate revelation, and added these remarkable words: "When thou movest one of thy limbs, is it moved by thy own power? Certainly not; for this limb is often sensible to involuntary motions. Consequently He who created thy body gives motion to this earthly tabernacle. And are the several ideas of which thy soul receives the impression formed by thyself? Much less are they, since these pour in upon thy mind whether thou wilt or no; consequently thou receivest thy ideas from Him who created thy soul. But as He leaves thy affections at full liberty, He gives thy mind such ideas as thy affections may deserve; if thou livest in God, thou actest, thou thinkest in God. After this thou needest only but open thine eyes to that light which enlightens all mankind, and it is then thou wilt perceive the truth, and make others perceive it." "Why, this," said I, "is Malebranche's doctrine to a tittle." "I am acquainted with thy Malebranche," said he; "he had something of the Friend in him, but was not enough so." These are the most considerable particulars I learned concerning the doctrine of the Quakers. In my next letter I shall acquaint you with their history, which you will find more singular than their opinions.

Letters on the English; or Lettres Philosophiques

Letter III: On The Quakers

You have already heard that the Quakers date from Christ, who, according to them, was the first Quaker. Religion, say these, was corrupted a little after His death, and remained in that state of corruption about sixteen hundred years. But there were always a few Quakers concealed in the world, who carefully preserved the sacred fire, which was extinguished in all but themselves, until at last this light spread itself in England in 1642.

It was at the time when Great Britain was torn to pieces by the intestine wars which three or four sects had raised in the name of God, that one George Fox, born in Leicestershire, and son to a silk weaver, took it into his head to preach, and, as he pretended, with all the requisites of a true apostle–that is, without being able either to read or write. He was about twenty-five years of age, irreproachable in his life and conduct, and a holy madman. He was equipped in leather from head to foot, and travelled from one village to another, exclaiming against war and the clergy. Had his invectives been levelled against the soldiery only he would have been safe enough, but he inveighed against ecclesiastics. Fox was seized at Derby, and being carried before a justice of peace, he did not once offer to pull off his leathern hat, upon which an officer gave him a great box of the ear, and cried to him, "Don't you know you are to appear uncovered before his worship?" Fox presented his other cheek to the officer, and begged him to give him another box for God's sake. The justice would have had him sworn before he asked him any questions. "Know, friend," says Fox to him, "that I never swear." The justice, observing he "thee'd" and "thou'd" him, sent him to the House of Correction, in Derby, with orders that he should be whipped there. Fox praised the Lord all the way he went to the House of Correction, where the justice's order was executed with the utmost severity. The men who whipped this enthusiast were greatly surprised to hear him beseech them to give him a few more lashes for the good of his soul. There was no need of entreating these people; the lashes were repeated, for which Fox thanked them very cordially, and began to preach. At first the spectators fell a-laughing, but they afterwards listened to him; and as enthusiasm is an epidemical distemper, many were persuaded, and those who scourged him became his first disciples. Being set at liberty, he ran up and down the country with a dozen proselytes at his heels, still declaiming against the clergy, and was whipped from time to time. Being one day set in the pillory, he harangued the crowd in so strong and moving a manner, that fifty of the auditors became his converts, and he won the rest so much in his favour that, his head being freed tumultuously from the hole where it was fastened, the populace went and searched for the Church of England clergyman who had been chiefly instrumental in bringing him to this punishment, and set him on the same pillory where Fox had stood.

Fox was bold enough to convert some of Oliver Cromwell's soldiers, who thereupon quitted the service and refused to take the oaths. Oliver, having as great a contempt for a sect which would not allow its members to fight, as Sixtus Quintus had for another sect, Dove non si chiavava, began to persecute these new converts. The prisons were crowded with them, but persecution seldom has any other effect than to increase the number of proselytes. These came, therefore, from their confinement more strongly confirmed in the principles they had imbibed, and followed by their gaolers, whom they had brought over to their belief. But the circumstances which contributed chiefly to the spreading of this sect were as follows:–Fox thought himself inspired, and consequently was of opinion that he must speak in a manner different from the rest of mankind. He thereupon began to writhe his body, to screw up his face, to hold in his breath, and to exhale it in a forcible manner, insomuch that the priestess of the Pythian god at Delphos could not have acted her part to better advantage. Inspiration soon became so habitual to him that he could scarce deliver himself in any other manner. This was the first gift he communicated to his disciples. These aped very sincerely their master's several grimaces, and shook in every limb the instant the fit of inspiration came upon them, whence they were called Quakers. The vulgar attempted to mimic them; they trembled, they spake through the nose, they quaked and fancied themselves inspired by the Holy Ghost. The only thing now wanting was a few miracles, and accordingly they wrought some.

Fox, this modern patriarch, spoke thus to a justice of peace before a large assembly of people: "Friend, take care what thou dost; God will soon punish thee for persecuting His saints." This magistrate, being one who besotted himself every day with bad beer and brandy, died of an appolexy two days after, the moment he had signed a mittimus for imprisoning some Quakers. The sudden death with which this justice was seized was not ascribed to his intemperance, but was universally looked upon as the effect of the holy man's predictions; so that this accident made more converts to Quakerism than a thousand sermons and as many shaking fits could have done. Oliver, finding them increase daily, was desirous of bringing them over to his party, and for that purpose attempted to bribe them by money. However, they were incorruptible, which made him one day declared that this religion was the only one he had ever met with that had resisted the charms of gold.

The Quakers were several times persecuted under Charles II.; not upon a religious account, but for refusing to pay the tithes, for "theeing" and "thouing" the magistrates, and for refusing to take the oaths enacted by the laws.

At last Robert Barclay, a native of Scotland, presented to the King, in 1675, his "Apology for the Quakers," a work as well drawn up as the subject could possibly admit. The dedication to Charles II. is not filled with mean, flattering encomiums, but abounds with bold touches in favour of truth and with the wisest counsels. "Thou hast tasted," said he to the King at the close of his epistle dedicatory, "of prosperity and adversity; thou knowest what it is to be banished thy native country; to be overruled as well as to rule and sit upon the throne; and, being oppressed, thou hast reason to know how hateful the oppressor is both to God and man. If, after all these warnings and advertisements, thou dost not turn unto the Lord with all thy heart, but forget Him who remembered thee in thy distress, and give up thyself to follow lust and vanity, surely great will be thy condemnation.

"Against which snare, as well as the temptation of those that may or do feed thee and prompt thee to evil, the most excellent and prevalent remedy will be, to apply thyself to that light of Christ which shineth in thy conscience, which neither can nor will flatter thee nor suffer thee to be at ease in thy sins, but doth and will deal plainly and faithfully with thee, as those that are followers thereof have plainly done.–Thy faithful friend and subject, Robert Barclay."

A more surprising circumstance is, that this epistle, written by a private man of no figure, was so happy in its effects, as to put a stop to the persecution.

Letters on the English; or Lettres Philosophiques

Letter IV: On The Quakers

About this time arose the illustrious William Penn, who established the power of the Quakers in America, and would have made them appear venerable in the eyes of the Europeans, were it possible for mankind to respect virtue when revealed in a ridiculous light. He was the only son of Vice-Admiral Penn, favourite of the Duke of York, afterwards King James II.

William Penn, at twenty years of age, happening to meet with a Quaker in Cork, whom he had known at Oxford, this man made a proselyte of him; and William being a sprightly youth, and naturally eloquent, having a winning aspect, and a very engaging carriage, he soon gained over some of his intimates. He carried matters so far, that he formed by insensible degrees a society of young Quakers, who met at his house; so that he was at the head of a sect when a little above twenty.

Being returned, after his leaving Cork, to the Vice-Admiral his father, instead of falling upon his knees to ask his blessing, he went up to him with his hat on, and said, "Friend, I am very glad to see thee in good health." The Vice-Admiral imagined his son to be crazy, but soon finding he was turned Quaker, he employed all the methods that prudence could suggest to engage him to behave and act like other people. The youth made no other answer to his father, than by exhorting him to turn Quaker also. At last his father confined himself to this single request, viz., "that he should wait upon the King and the Duke of York with his hat under his arm, and should not 'thee' and 'thou' them." William answered, "that he could not do these things, for conscience' sake," which exasperated his father to such a degree, that he turned him out of doors. Young Penn gave God thanks for permitting him so suffer to early in His cause, after which he went into the city, where he held forth, and made a great number of converts.

The Church of England clergy found their congregations dwindle away, daily; and Penn being young, handsome, and of a graceful stature, the court as well as the city ladies flocked very devoutly to his meeting. The patriarch, George Fox, hearing of his great reputation, came to London (though the journey was very long) purely to see and converse with him. Both resolved to go upon missions into foreign countries, and accordingly they embarked for Holland, after having left labourers sufficient to take care of the London vineyard.

Letters on the English; or Lettres Philosophiques

Their labours were crowned with success in Amsterdam, but a circumstance which reflected the greatest honour on them, and at the same time put their humility to the greatest trial, was the reception they met with from Elizabeth, the Princess Palatine, aunt to George I. of Great Britain, a lady conspicuous for her genius and knowledge, and to whom Descartes had dedicated his Philosophical Romance.

She was then retired to The Hague, where she received these Friends, for so the Quakers were at that time called in Holland. This princess had several conferences with them in her palace, and she at last entertained so favourable an opinion of Quakerism, that they confessed she was not far from the kingdom of heaven. The Friends sowed likewise the good seed in Germany, but reaped very little fruit; for the mode of "theeing" and "thouing" was not approved of in a country where a man is perpetually obliged to employ the titles of "highness" and "excellency." William Penn returned soon to England upon hearing of his father's sickness, in order to see him before he died. The Vice-Admiral was reconciled to his son, and though of a different persuasion, embraced him tenderly. William made a fruitless exhortation to his father not to receive the sacrament, but to die a Quaker, and the good old man entreated his son William to wear buttons on his sleeves, and a crape hatband in his beaver, but all to no purpose.

William Penn inherited very large possessions, part of which consisted in Crown debts due to the Vice-Admiral for sums he had advanced for the sea service. No moneys were at that time more insecure than those owing from the king. Penn was obliged to go more than once, and "thee" and "thou" King Charles and his Ministers, in order to recover the debt, and at last, instead of specie, the Government, invested him with the right and sovereignty of a province of America, to the south of Maryland. Thus was a Quaker raised to sovereign power. Penn set sail for his new dominions with two ships freighted with Quakers, who followed his fortune. The country was then called Pennsylvania from William Penn, who there founded Philadelphia, now the most flourishing city in that country. The first step he took was to enter into an alliance with his American neighbours, and this is the only treaty between those people and the Christians that was not ratified by an oath, and was never infringed. The new sovereign was at the same time the legislator of Pennsylvania, and enacted very wise and prudent laws, none of which have ever been changed since his time. The first is, to injure no person upon a religious account, and to consider as brethren all those who believe in one God.

Letters on the English; or Lettres Philosophiques

He had no sooner settled his government, but several American merchants came and peopled this colony. The natives of the country, instead of flying into the woods, cultivated by insensible degrees a friendship with the peaceable Quakers. They loved these foreigners as much as they detested the other Christians who had conquered and laid waste America. In a little time a great number of these savages (falsely so called), charmed with the mild and gentle disposition of their neighbours, came in crowds to William Penn, and besought him to admit them into the number of his vassals. It was very rare and uncommon for a sovereign to be "thee'd" and "thou'd" by the meanest of his subjects, who never took their hats off when they came into his presence; and as singular for a Government to be without one priest in it, and for a people to be without arms, either offensive or defensive; for a body of citizens to be absolutely undistinguished but by the public employments, and for neighbours not to entertain the least jealousy one against the other.

William Penn might glory in having brought down upon earth the so much boasted golden age, which in all probability never existed but in Pennsylvania. He returned to England to settle some affairs relating to his new dominions. After the death of King Charles II., King James, who had loved the father, indulged the same affection to the son, and no longer considered him as an obscure sectary, but as a very great man. The king's politics on this occasion agreed with his inclinations. He was desirous of pleasing the Quakers by annulling the laws made against Nonconformists, in order to have an opportunity, by this universal toleration, of establishing the Romish religion. All the sectarists in England saw the snare that was laid for them, but did not give into it; they never failing to unite when the Romish religion, their common enemy, is to be opposed. But Penn did not think himself bound in any manner to renounce his principles, merely to favour Protestants to whom he was odious, in opposition to a king who loved him. He had established a universal toleration with regard to conscience in America, and would not have it thought that he intended to destroy it in Europe, for which reason he adhered so inviolably to King James, that a report prevailed universally of his being a Jesuit. This calumny affected him very strongly, and he was obliged to justify himself in print. However, the unfortunate King James II., in whom, as in most princes of the Stuart family, grandeur and weakness were equally blended, and who, like them, as much overdid some things as he was short in others, lost his kingdom in a manner that is hardly to be accounted for.

Letters on the English; or Lettres Philosophiques

All the English sectarists accepted from William III. and his Parliament the toleration and indulgence which they had refused when offered by King James. It was then the Quakers began to enjoy, by virtue of the laws, the several privileges they possess at this time. Penn having at last seen Quakerism firmly established in his native country, went back to Pennsylvania. His own people and the Americans received him with tears of joy, as though he had been a father who was returned to visit his children. All the laws had been religiously observed in his absence, a circumstance in which no legislator had ever been happy but himself. After having resided some years in Pennsylvania he left it, but with great reluctance, in order to return to England, there to solicit some matters in favour of the commerce of Pennsylvania. But he never saw it again, he dying in Ruscombe, in Berkshire, in 1718.

I am not able to guess what fate Quakerism may have in America, but I perceive it dwindles away daily in England. In all countries where liberty of conscience is allowed, the established religion will at last swallow up all the rest. Quakers are disqualified from being members of Parliament; nor can they enjoy any post or preferment, because an oath must always be taken on these occasions, and they never swear. They are therefore reduced to the necessity of subsisting upon traffic. Their children, whom the industry of their parents has enriched, are desirous of enjoying honours, of wearing buttons and ruffles; and quite ashamed of being called Quakers they become converts to the Church of England, merely to be in the fashion.

Letter V: On The Church Of England

England is properly the country of sectarists. Multae sunt mansiones in domo patris mei (in my Father's house are many mansions). An Englishman, as one to whom liberty is natural, may go to heaven his own way.

Nevertheless, though every one is permitted to serve God in whatever mode or fashion he thinks proper, yet their true religion, that in which a man makes his fortune, is the sect of Episcopalians or Churchmen, called the Church of England, or simply the Church, by way of eminence. No person can possess an employment either in England or Ireland unless he be ranked among the faithful, that is, professes himself a member of the Church of England. This reason (which carries mathematical evidence with it) has converted such numbers of Dissenters of all persuasions, that not a twentieth part of the nation is out of the pale of the Established Church. The English clergy have retained a great number of the Romish ceremonies, and especially that of receiving, with a most scrupulous attention, their tithes. They also have the pious ambition to aim at superiority.

Moreover, they inspire very religiously their flock with a holy zeal against Dissenters of all denominations. This zeal was pretty violent under the Tories in the four last years of Queen Anne; but was productive of no greater mischief than the breaking the windows of some meeting-houses and the demolishing of a few of them. For religious rage ceased in England with the civil wars, and was no more under Queen Anne than the hollow noise of a sea whose billows still heaved, though so long after the storm when the Whigs and Tories laid waste their native country, in the same manner as the Guelphs and Ghibellines formerly did theirs. It was absolutely necessary for both parties to call in religion on this occasion; the Tories declared for Episcopacy, and the Whigs, as some imagined, were for abolishing it; however, after these had got the upper hand, they contented themselves with only abridging it.

At the time when the Earl of Oxford and the Lord Bolingbroke used to drink healths to the Tories, the Church of England considered these noblemen as the defenders of its holy privileges. The lower House of Convocation (kind of House of Commons) composed wholly of the clergy, was in some credit at that time; at least the members of it had the liberty to meet, to dispute on ecclesiastical matters, to sentence impious books from time to time to the flames, that is, books written against themselves. The Ministry which is now composed of Whigs does not so much as allow those gentlemen to assemble, so that they are at this time reduced (in the obscurity of their respective parishes) to the melancholy occupation of praying for the prosperity of the Government whose tranquility they would willingly disturb. With regard to the bishops, who are twenty-six in all, they still have seats in the House of Lords in spite of the Whigs, because the ancient abuse of considering them as barons subsists to this day. There is a clause, however, in the oath which the Government requires from these gentlemen, that puts their Christian patience to a very great trial, viz., that they shall be of the Church of England as by law established. There are few bishops, deans, or other dignitaries, but imagine they are so jure divino; it is consequently a great mortification to them to be obliged to confess that they owe their dignity to a pitiful law enacted by a set of profane laymen. A learned monk (Father Courayer) wrote a book lately to prove the validity and succession of English ordinations. This book was forbid in France, but do you believe that the English Ministry were pleased with it? Far from it. Those damned Whigs don't care a straw whether the episcopal succession among them hath been interrupted or not, or whether Bishop Parker was consecrated (as it is pretended) in a tavern or a church; for these Whigs are much better pleased that the Bishops should derive their authority from the Parliament than from the Apostles. The Lord Bolingbroke observed that this notion of divine right would only make so many tyrants in lawn sleeves, but that the laws made so many citizens.

With regard to the morals of the English clergy, they are more regular than those of France, and for this reason. All the clergy (a very few excepted) are educated in the Universities of Oxford or Cambridge, far from the depravity and corruption which reign in the capital. They are not called to dignities till very late, at a time of life when men are sensible of no other passion but avarice, that is, when their ambition craves a supply. Employments are here bestowed both in the Church and the army, as a reward for long services; and we never see youngsters made bishops or colonels immediately upon their laying aside the academical gown; and besides most of the clergy are married. The stiff and awkward air contracted by them at the University, and the little familiarity the men of this country have with the ladies, commonly oblige a bishop to confine himself to, and rest contented with, his own. Clergymen sometimes take a glass at the tavern, custom giving them a sanction on this occasion; and if they fuddle themselves it is in a very serious manner, and without giving the least scandal.

That fable–mixed kind of mortal (not to be defined), who is neither of the clergy nor of the laity; in a word, the thing called Abbe in France; is a species quite unknown in England. All the clergy here are very much upon the reserve, and most of them pedants. When these are told that in France young fellows famous for their dissoluteness, and raised to the highest dignities of the Church by female intrigues, address the fair publicly in an amorous way, amuse themselves in writing tender love songs, entertain their friends very splendidly every night at their own houses, and after the banquet is ended withdraw to invoke the assistance of the Holy Ghost, and call themselves boldly the successors of the Apostles, they bless God for their being Protestants. But these are shameless heretics, who deserve to be blown hence through the flames to old Nick, as Rabelais says, and for this reason I don't trouble myself about them.

Letters on the English; or Lettres Philosophiques

Letter VI: On The Presbyterians

The Church of England is confined almost to the kingdom whence it received its name, and to Ireland, for Presbyterianism is the established religion in Scotland. This Presbyterianism is directly the same with Calvinism, as it was established in France, and is now professed at Geneva. As the priests of this sect receive but very inconsiderable stipends from their churches, and consequently cannot emulate the splendid luxury of bishops, they exclaim very naturally against honours which they can never attain to. Figure to yourself the haughty Diogenes trampling under foot the pride of Plato. The Scotch Presbyterians are not very unlike that proud though tattered reasoner. Diogenes did not use Alexander half so impertinently as these treated King Charles II.; for when they took up arms in his cause in opposition to Oliver, who had deceived them, they forced that poor monarch to undergo the hearing of three or four sermons every day, would not suffer him to play, reduced him to a state of penitence and mortification, so that Charles soon grew sick of these pedants, and accordingly eloped from them with as much joy as a youth does from school.

A Church of England minister appears as another Cato in presence of a juvenile, sprightly French graduate, who bawls for a whole morning together in the divinity schools, and hums a song in chorus with ladies in the evening; but this Cato is a very spark when before a Scotch Presbyterian. The latter affects a serious gait, puts on a sour look, wears a vastly broad−brimmed hat and a long cloak over a very short coat, preaches through the nose, and gives the name of the whore of Babylon to all churches where the ministers are so fortunate as to enjoy an annual revenue of five or six thousand pounds, and where the people are weak enough to suffer this, and to give them the titles of my lord, your lordship, or your eminence.

These gentlemen, who have also some churches in England, introduced there the mode of grave and severe exhortations. To them is owing the sanctification of Sunday in the three kingdoms. People are there forbidden to work or take any recreation on that day, in which the severity is twice as great as that of the Romish Church. No operas, plays, or concerts are allowed in London on Sundays, and even cards are so expressly forbidden that none but persons of quality, and those we call the genteel, play on that day; the rest of the nation go either to church, to the tavern, or to see their mistresses.

Letters on the English; or Lettres Philosophiques

Though the Episcopal and Presbyterian sects are the two prevailing ones in Great Britain, yet all others are very welcome to come and settle in it, and live very sociably together, though most of their preachers hate one another almost as cordially as a Jansenist damns a Jesuit.

Take a view of the Royal Exchange in London, a place more venerable than many courts of justice, where the representatives of all nations meet for the benefit of mankind. There the Jew, the Mahometan, and the Christian transact together, as though they all professed the same religion, and give the name of infidel to none but bankrupts. There thee Presbyterian confides in the Anabaptist, and the Churchman depends on the Quaker's word. At the breaking up of this pacific and free assembly, some withdraw to the synagogue, and others to take a glass. This man goes and is baptized in a great tub, in the name of the Father, Son, and Holy Ghost: that man has his son's foreskin cut off, whilst a set of Hebrew words (quite unintelligible to him) are mumbled over his child. Others retire to their churches, and there wait for the inspiration of heaven with their hats on, and all are satisfied.

If one religion only were allowed in England, the Government would very possibly become arbitrary; if there were but two, the people would cut one another's throats; but as there are such a multitude, they all live happy and in peace.

Letter VII: On The Socinians, Or Arians, Or Antitrinitarians

There is a little sect here composed of clergymen, and of a few very learned person among the laity, who, though they don't call themselves Arians or Socinians, do yet dissent entirely from St. Athanasius with regard to their notions of the Trinity, and declare very frankly that the Father is greater than the Son.

Do you remember what is related of a certain orthodox bishop, who in order to convince an emperor of the reality of consubstantiation, put his hand under the chin of the monarch's son, and took him by the nose in presence of his sacred majesty? The emperor was going to order his attendants to throw the bishop out of the window, when the good old man gave him this handsome and convincing reason: "Since your majesty," said he, "is angry when your son has not due respect shown him, what punishment do you think will God the Father inflict on those who refuse His Son Jesus the titles due to Him?" The

Letters on the English; or Lettres Philosophiques

persons I just now mentioned declare that the holy bishop took a very wrong step, that his argument was inconclusive, and that the emperor should have answered him thus: "Know that there are two ways by which men may be wanting in respect to me—first, in not doing honour sufficient to my son; and, secondly, in paying him the same honour as to me."

Be this as it will, the principles of Arius begin to revive, not only in England, but in Holland and Poland. The celebrated Sir Isaac Newton honoured this opinion so far as to countenance it. This philosopher thought that the Unitarians argued more mathematically than we do. But the most sanguine stickler for Arianism is the illustrious Dr. Clark. This man is rigidly virtuous, and of a mild disposition, is more fond of his tenets than desirous of propagating them, and absorbed so entirely in problems and calculations that he is a mere reasoning machine.

It is he who wrote a book which is much esteemed and little understood, on the existence of God, and another, more intelligible, but pretty much contemned, on the truth of the Christian religion. He never engaged in scholastic disputes, which our friend calls venerable trifles. He only published a work containing all the testimonies of the primitive ages for and against the Unitarians, and leaves to the reader the counting of the voices and the liberty of forming a judgment. This book won the doctor a great number of partisans, and lost him the See of Canterbury but, in my humble opinion, he was out in his calculation, and had better have been Primate of all England than merely an Arian parson.

You see that opinions are subject to revolutions as well as empires. Arianism, after having triumphed during three centuries, and been forgot twelve, rises at last out of its own ashes; but it has chosen a very improper season to make its appearance in, the present age being quite cloyed with disputes and sects. The members of this sect are, besides, too few to be indulged the liberty of holding public assemblies, which, however, they will, doubtless, be permitted to do in case they spread considerably. But people are now so very cold with respect to all things of this kind, that there is little probability any new religion, or old one, that may be revived, will meet with favour. Is it not whimsical enough that Luther, Calvin, and Zuinglius, all of 'em wretched authors, should have founded sects which are now spread over a great part of Europe, that Mahomet, though so ignorant, should have given a religion to Asia and Africa, and that Sir Isaac Newton, Dr. Clark, Mr. Locke, Mr. Le Clerc, etc., the greatest philosophers, as well as the ablest writers of their ages, should scarce have been able to raise a little flock, which even decreases daily.

This it is to be born at a proper period of time. Were Cardinal de Retz to return again into the world neither his eloquence nor his intrigues would draw together ten women in Paris. Were Oliver Cromwell, he who beheaded his sovereign, and seized upon the kingly dignity, to rise from the dead, he would be a wealthy City trader, and no more.

Letter VIII: On The Parliament

The members of the English Parliament are fond of comparing themselves to the old Romans.

Not long since Mr. Shippen opened a speech in the House of Commons with these words, "The majesty of the people of England would be wounded." The singularity of the expression occasioned a loud laugh; but this gentleman, so far from being disconcerted, repeated the same words with a resolute tone of voice, and the laugh ceased. In my opinion, the majesty of the people of England has nothing in common with that of the people of Rome, much less is there any affinity between their Governments. There is in London a senate, some of the members whereof are accused (doubtless very unjustly) of selling their voices on certain occasions, as was done in Rome; this is the only resemblance. Besides, the two nations appear to me quite opposite in character, with regard both to good and evil. The Romans never knew the dreadful folly of religious wars, an abomination reserved for devout preachers of patience and humility. Marious and Sylla, Caesar and Pompey, Anthony and Augustus, did not draw their swords and set the world in a blaze merely to determine whether the flamen should wear his shirt over his robe, or his robe over his shirt, or whether the sacred chickens should eat and drink, or eat only, in order to take the augury. The English have hanged one another by law, and cut one another to pieces in pitched battles, for quarrels of as trifling nature. The sects of the Episcopalians and Presbyterians quite distracted these very serious heads for a time. But I fancy they will hardly ever be so silly again, they seeming to be grown wiser at their own expense; and I do not perceive the least inclination in them to murder one another merely about syllogisms, as some zealots among them once did.

Letters on the English; or Lettres Philosophiques

But here follows a more essential difference between Rome and England, which gives the advantage entirely to the later—viz., that the civil wars of Rome ended in slavery, and those of the English in liberty. The English are the only people upon earth who have been able to prescribe limits to the power of kings by resisting them; and who, by a series of struggles, have at last established that wise Government where the Prince is all powerful to do good, and, at the same time, is restrained from committing evil; where the nobles are great without insolence, though there are no vassals; and where the people share in the Government without confusion.

The House of Lords and that of the Commons divide the legislative power under the king, but the Romans had no such balance. The patricians and plebeians in Rome were perpetually at variance, and there was no intermediate power to reconcile them. The Roman senate, who were so unjustly, so criminally proud as not to suffer the plebeians to share with them in anything, could find no other artifice to keep the latter out of the administration than by employing them in foreign wars. They considered the plebeians as a wild beast, whom it behoved them to let loose upon their neighbours, for fear they should devour their masters. Thus the greatest defect in the Government of the Romans raised them to be conquerors. By being unhappy at home, they triumphed over and possessed themselves of the world, till at last their divisions sunk them to slavery.

The Government of England will never rise to so exalted a pitch of glory, nor will its end be so fatal. The English are not fired with the splendid folly of making conquests, but would only prevent their neighbours from conquering. They are not only jealous of their own liberty, but even of that of other nations. The English were exasperated against Louis XIV. for no other reason but because he was ambitious, and declared war against him merely out of levity, not from any interested motives.

The English have doubtless purchased their liberties at a very high price, and waded through seas of blood to drown the idol of arbitrary power. Other nations have been involved in as great calamities, and have shed as much blood; but then the blood they split in defence of their liberties only enslaved them the more.

That which rises to a revolution in England is no more than a sedition in other countries. A city in Spain, in Barbary, or in Turkey, takes up arms in defence of its privileges, when immediately it is stormed by mercenary troops, it is punished by executioners, and the rest of the nation kiss the chains they are loaded with. The French are of opinion that the government of this island is more tempestuous than the sea which surrounds it, which indeed is true; but then it is never so but when the king raises the storm— when he attempts to seize the ship of which he is only the chief pilot. The civil wars of France lasted longer, were more cruel, and productive of greater evils than those of England; but none of these civil wars had a wise and prudent liberty for their object.

In the detestable reigns of Charles IX. and Henry III. the whole affair was only whether the people should be slaves to the Guises. With regard to the last war of Paris, it deserves only to be hooted at. Methinks I see a crowd of schoolboys rising up in arms against their master, and afterwards whipped for it. Cardinal de Retz, who was witty and brave (but to no purpose), rebellious without a cause, factious without design, and head of a defenseless party, caballed for caballing's sake, and seemed to foment the civil war merely out of diversion. The parliament did not know what he intended, nor what he did not intend. He levied troops by Act of Parliament, and the next moment cashiered them. He threatened, he begged pardon; he set a price upon Cardinal Mazarin's head, and afterwards congratulated him in a public manner. Our civil wars under Charles VI. were bloody and cruel, those of the League execrable, and that of the Frondeurs ridiculous.

That for which the French chiefly reproach the English nation is the murder of King Charles I., whom his subjects treated exactly as he would have treated them had his reign been prosperous. After all, consider on one side Charles I., defeated in a pitched battle, imprisoned, tried, sentenced to die in Westminster Hall, and then beheaded. And on the other, the Emperor Henry VII., poisoned by his chaplain at his receiving the Sacrament; Henry III. stabbed by a monk; thirty assassinations projected against Henry IV., several of them put in execution, and the last bereaving that great monarch of his life. Weigh, I say, all these wicked attempts and then judge.

Letter IX: On The Government

That mixture in the English Government, that harmony between King, Lords, and Commons, did not always subsist. England was enslaved for a long series of years by the Romans, the Saxons, the Danes, and the French successively. William the Conqueror particularly, ruled them with a rod of iron. He disposed as absolutely of the lives and fortunes of his conquered subjects as an eastern monarch; and forbade, upon pain of death, the English either fire or candle in their houses after eight o'clock; whether he did

Letters on the English; or Lettres Philosophiques

this to prevent their nocturnal meetings, or only to try, by this odd and whimsical prohibition, how far it was possible for one man to extend his power over his fellow-creatures. It is true, indeed, that the English had Parliaments before and after William the Conqueror, and they boast of them, as though these assemblies then called Parliaments, composed of ecclesiastical tyrants and of plunderers entitled barons, had been the guardians of the public liberty and happiness.

The barbarians who came from the shores of the Baltic, and settled in the rest of Europe, brought with them the form of government called States or Parliaments, about which so much noise is made, and which are so little understood. Kings, indeed, were not absolute in those days; but then the people were more wretched upon that very account, and more completely enslaved. The chiefs of these savages, who had laid waste France, Italy, Spain, and England, made themselves monarchs. Their generals divided among themselves the several countries they had conquered, whence sprung those margraves, those peers, those barons, those petty tyrants, who often contested with their sovereigns for the spoils of whole nations. These were birds of prey fighting with an eagle for doves whose blood the victorious was to suck. Every nation, instead of being governed by one master, was trampled upon by a hundred tyrants. The priests soon played a part among them. Before this it had been the fate of the Gauls, the Germans, and the Britons, to be always governed by their Druids and the chiefs of their villages, an ancient kind of barons, not so tyrannical as their successors. These Druids pretended to be mediators between God and man. They enacted laws, they fulminated their excommunications, and sentenced to death. The bishops succeeded, by insensible degrees, to their temporal authority in the Goth and Vandal government. The popes set themselves at their head, and armed with their briefs, their bulls, and reinforced by monks, they made even kings tremble, deposed and assassinated them at pleasure, and employed every artifice to draw into their own purses moneys from all parts of Europe. The weak Ina, one of the tyrants of the Saxon Heptarchy in England, was the first monarch who submitted, in his pilgrimage to Rome, to pay St. Peter's penny (equivalent very near to a French crown) for every house in his dominions. The whole island soon followed his example; England became insensibly one of the Pope's provinces, and the Holy Father used to send from time to time his legates thither to levy exorbitant taxes. At last King John delivered up by a public instrument the kingdom of England to the Pope, who had excommunicated him; but the barons, not finding their account in this resignation, dethroned the wretched King John and seated Louis, father to St. Louis, King of France, in his place. However, they were soon weary of their new monarch, and accordingly obliged him to return to France.

Letters on the English; or Lettres Philosophiques

Whilst that the barons, the bishops, and the popes, all laid waste England, where all were for ruling; the most numerous, the most useful, even the most virtuous, and consequently the most venerable part of mankind, consisting of those who study the laws and the sciences, of traders, of artificers, in a word, of all who were not tyrants—that is, those who are called the people: these, I say, were by them looked upon as so many animals beneath the dignity of the human species. The Commons in those ages were far from sharing in the government, they being villains or peasants, whose labour, whose blood, were the property of their masters who entitled themselves the nobility. The major part of men in Europe were at that time what they are to this day in several parts of the world—they were villains or bondsmen of lords—that is, a kind of cattle bought and sold with the land. Many ages passed away before justice could be done to human nature—before mankind were conscious that it was abominable for many to sow, and but few reap. And was not France very happy, when the power and authority of those petty robbers was abolished by the lawful authority of kings and of the people?

Happily, in the violent shocks which the divisions between kings and the nobles gave to empires, the chains of nations were more or less heavy. Liberty in England sprang from the quarrels of tyrants. The barons forced King John and King Henry III. to grant the famous Magna Charta, the chief design of which was indeed to make kings dependent on the Lords; but then the rest of the nation were a little favoured in it, in order that they might join on proper occasions with their pretended masters. This great Charter, which is considered as the sacred origin of the English liberties, shows in itself how little liberty was known.

The title alone proves that the king thought he had a just right to be absolute; and that the barons, and even the clergy, forced him to give up the pretended right, for no other reason but because they were the most powerful.

Magna Charta begins in this style: "We grant, of our own free will, the following privileges to the archbishops, bishops, priors, and barons of our kingdom," etc.

The House of Commons is not once mentioned in the articles of this Charter—a proof that it did not yet exist, or that it existed without power. Mention is therein made, by name, of the freemen of England—a melancholy proof that some were not so. It appears, by Article XXXII., that these pretended freemen owed service to their lords. Such a liberty as this was not many removes from slavery.

Letters on the English; or Lettres Philosophiques

By Article XXI., the king ordains that his officers shall not henceforward seize upon, unless they pay for them, the horses and carts of freemen. The people considered this ordinance as a real liberty, though it was a greater tyranny. Henry VII., that happy usurper and great politician, who pretended to love the barons, though he in reality hated and feared them, got their lands alienated. By this means the villains, afterwards acquiring riches by their industry, purchased the estates and country seats of the illustrious peers who had ruined themselves by their folly and extravagance, and all the lands got by insensible degrees into other hands.

The power of the House of Commons increased every day. The families of the ancient peers were at last extinct; and as peers only are properly noble in England, there would be no such thing in strictness of law as nobility in that island, had not the kings created new barons from time to time, and preserved the body of peers, once a terror to them, to oppose them to the Commons, since become so formidable.

All these new peers who compose the Higher House receive nothing but their titles from the king, and very few of them have estates in those places whence they take their titles. One shall be Duke of D—, though he has not a foot of land in Dorsetshire; and another is Earl of a village, though he scarce knows where it is situated. The peers have power, but it is only in the Parliament House.

There is no such thing here as haute, moyenne, and basse justice—that is, a power to judge in all matters civil and criminal; nor a right or privilege of hunting in the grounds of a citizen, who at the same time is not permitted to fire a gun in his own field.

No one is exempted in this country from paying certain taxes because he is a nobleman or a priest. All duties and taxes are settled by the House of Commons, whose power is greater than that of the Peers, though inferior to it in dignity. The spiritual as well as temporal Lords have the liberty to reject a Money Bill brought in by the Commons; but they are not allowed to alter anything in it, and must either pass or throw it out without restriction. When the Bill has passed the Lords and is signed by the king, then the whole nation pays, every man in proportion to his revenue or estate, not according to his title, which would be absurd. There is no such thing as an arbitrary subsidy or poll-tax, but a real tax on the lands, of all which an estimate was made in the reign of the famous King William III.

Letters on the English; or Lettres Philosophiques

The land-tax continues still upon the same foot, though the revenue of the lands is increased. Thus no one is tyrannised over, and every one is easy. The feet of the peasants are not bruised by wooden shoes; they eat white bread, are well clothed, and are not afraid of increasing their stock of cattle, nor of tiling their houses from any apprehension that their taxes will be raised the year following. The annual income of the estates of a great many commoners in England amounts to two hundred thousand livres, and yet these do not think it beneath them to plough the lands which enrich them, and on which they enjoy their liberty.

Letter X: On Trade

As trade enriched the citizens in England, so it contributed to their freedom, and this freedom on the other side extended their commerce, whence arose the grandeur of the State. Trade raised by insensible degrees the naval power, which gives the English a superiority over the seas, and they now are masters of very near two hundred ships of war. Posterity will very probably be surprised to hear that an island whose only produce is a little lead, tin, fuller's-earth, and coarse wool, should become so powerful by its commerce, as to be able to send, in 1723, three fleets at the same time to three different and far distanced parts of the globe. One before Gibraltar, conquered and still possessed by the English; a second to Porto Bello, to dispossess the King of Spain of the treasures of the West Indies; and a third into the Baltic, to prevent the Northern Powers from coming to an engagement.

At the time when Louis XIV. made all Italy tremble, and that his armies, which had already possessed themselves of Savoy and Piedmont, were upon the point of taking Turin; Prince Eugene was obliged to march from the middle of Germany in order to succour Savoy. Having no money, without which cities cannot be either taken or defended, he addressed himself to some English merchants. These, at an hour and a half's warning, lent him five millions, whereby he was enabled to deliver Turin, and to beat the French; after which he wrote the following short letter to the persons who had disbursed him the above-mentioned sums: "Gentlemen, I received your money, and flatter myself that I have laid it out to your satisfaction." Such a circumstance as this raises a just pride in an English merchant, and makes him presume (not without some reason) to compare himself to a Roman citizen; and, indeed, a peer's brother does not think traffic beneath him. When the Lord Townshend was Minister of State, a brother of his was content to be a City merchant; and at the time that the Earl of Oxford governed Great Britain, his younger brother was no more than a factor in Aleppo, where he chose to live, and where he died. This custom, which begins, however, to be laid aside, appears monstrous to Germans, vainly puffed up with their extraction. These think it morally impossible that the son of an English peer should be no more than a rich and powerful citizen, for all are princes in Germany. There have been thirty highnesses of the same name, all whose patrimony consisted only in their escutcheons and their pride.

In France the title of marquis is given gratis to any one who will accept of it; and whosoever arrives at Paris from the midst of the most remote provinces with money in his purse, and a name terminating in ac or ille, may strut about, and cry, "Such a man as I! A man of my rank and figure!" and may look down upon a trader with sovereign contempt; whilst the trader on the other side, by thus often hearing his profession treated so disdainfully, is fool enough to blush at it. However, I need not say which is most useful to a nation; a lord, powdered in the tip of the mode, who knows exactly at what o'clock the king rises and goes to bed, and who gives himself airs of grandeur and state, at the same time that he is acting the slave in the ante-chamber of a prime minister; or a merchant, who enriches his country, despatches orders from his counting-house to Surat and Grand Cairo, and contributes to the felicity of the world.

Letter XI: On Inoculation

It is inadvertently affirmed in the Christian countries of Europe that the English are fools and madmen. Fools, because they give their children the small-pox to prevent their catching it; and madmen, because they wantonly communicate a certain and dreadful distemper to their children, merely to prevent an uncertain evil. The English, on the other side, call the rest of the Europeans cowardly and unnatural. Cowardly, because they are afraid of putting their children to a little pain; unnatural, because they expose them to die one time or other of the small-pox. But that the reader may be able to judge whether the English or those who differ from them in opinion are in the right, here follows the history of the famed innoculation, which is mentioned with so much dread in France.

Letters on the English; or Lettres Philosophiques

The Circassian women have, from time immemorial, communicated the small-pox to their children when not above six months old by making an incision in the arm, and by putting into this incision a pustule, taken carefully from the body of another child. This pustule produces the same effect in the arm it is laid in as yeast in a piece of dough; it ferments, and diffuses through the whole mass of blood the qualities with which it is impregnated. The pustules of the child in whom the artificial small-pox has been thus inoculated are employed to communicate the same distemper to others. There is an almost perpetual circulation of it in Circassia; and when unhappily the small-pox has quite left the country, the inhabitants of it are in as great trouble and perplexity as other nations when their harvest has fallen short.

The circumstance that introduced a custom in Circassia, which appears so singular to others, is nevertheless a cause common to all nations, I mean maternal tenderness and interest.

The Circassians are poor, and their daughters are beautiful, and indeed, it is in them they chiefly trade. They furnish with beauties the seraglios of the Turkish Sultan, of the Persian Sophy, and of all those who are wealthy enough to purchase and maintain such precious merchandise. These maidens are very honourably and virtuously instructed to fondle and caress men; are taught dances of a very polite and effeminate kind; and how to heighten by the most voluptuous artifices the pleasures of their disdainful masters for whom they are designed. These unhappy creatures repeat their lesson to their mothers, in the same manner as little girls among us repeat their catechism without understanding one word they say.

Now it often happened that, after a father and mother had taken the utmost care of the education of their children, they were frustrated of all their hopes in an instant. The small-pox getting into the family, one daughter died of it, another lost an eye, a third had a great nose at her recovery, and the unhappy parents were completely ruined. Even, frequently, when the small-pox became epidemical, trade was suspended for several years, which thinned very considerably the seraglios of Persia and Turkey.

A trading nation is always watchful over its own interests, and grasps at every discovery that may be of advantage to its commerce. The Circassians observed that scarce one person in a thousand was ever attacked by a small-pox of a violent kind. That some, indeed, had this distemper very favourably three or four times, but never twice so as to prove fatal; in a word, that no one ever had it in a violent degree twice in his life. They observed farther, that when the small-pox is of the milder sort, and the pustules have only a tender, delicate skin to break through, they never leave the least scar in the face. From these natural observations they concluded, that in case an infant of six months or a year old should have a milder sort of small-pox, he would not die of it, would not be marked, nor be ever afflicted with it again.

In order, therefore, to preserve the life and beauty of their children, the only thing remaining was to give them the small-pox in their infant years. This they did by inoculating in the body of a child a pustule taken from the most regular and at the same time the most favourable sort of small-pox that could be procured.

The experiment could not possibly fail. The Turks, who are people of good sense, soon adopted this custom, insomuch that at this time there is not a bassa in Constantinople but communicates the small-pox to his children of both sexes immediately upon their being weaned.

Some pretend that the Circassians borrowed this custom anciently from the Arabians; but we shall leave the clearing up of this point of history to some learned Benedictine, who will not fail to compile a great many folios on this subject, with the several proofs or authorities. All I have to say upon it is that, in the beginning of the reign of King George I., the Lady Wortley Montague, a woman of as fine a genius, and endued with as great a strength of mind, as any of her sex in the British Kingdoms, being with her husband, who was ambassador at the Porte, made no scruple to communicate the small-pox to an infant of which she was delivered in Constantinople.

The chaplain represented to his lady, but to no purpose, that this was an un-Christian operation, and therefore that it could succeed with none but infidels. However, it had the most happy effect upon the son of the Lady Wortley Montague, who, at her return to England, communicated the experiment to the Princess of Wales, now Queen of England. It must be confessed that this princess, abstracted from her crown and titles, was born to encourage the whole circle of arts, and to do good to mankind. She appears as an amiable philosopher on the throne, having never let slip one opportunity of improving the great talents she received from Nature, nor of exerting her beneficence. It is she who, being informed that a daughter of Milton was living, but in miserable circumstances, immediately sent her a considerable present. It is she who protects the learned Father

Letters on the English; or Lettres Philosophiques

Courayer. It is she who condenscended to attempt a reconciliation between Dr. Clark and Mr. Leibnitz. The moment this princess heard of inoculation, she caused an experiment of it to be made on four criminals sentenced to die, and by that means preserved their lives doubly; for she not only saved them from the gallows, but by means of this artificial small-pox prevented their ever having that distemper in a natural way, with which they would very probably have been attacked one time on other, and might have died of in a more advanced age.

The princess being assured of the usefulness of this operation, caused her own children to be inoculated. A great part of the kingdom followed her example, and since that time ten thousand children, at least, of persons of condition owe in this manner their lives to her Majesty and to the Lady Wortley Montague; and as many of the fair sex are obliged to them for their beauty.

Upon a general calculation, threescore persons in every hundred have the small-pox. Of these threescore, twenty die of it in the most favourable season of life, and as many more wear the disagreeable remains of it in their faces so long as they live. Thus, a fifth part of mankind either die or are disfigured by this distemper. But it does not prove fatal to so much as one among those who are inoculated in Turkey or in England, unless the patient be infirm, or would have died had not the experiment been made upon him. Besides, no one is disfigured, no one had the small-pox a second time, if the inoculation was perfect. It is therefore certain, that had the lady of some French ambassador brought this secret from Constantinople to Paris, the nation would have been for ever obliged to her. Then the Duke de Villequier, father to the Duke d'Aumont, who enjoys the most vigorous constitution, and is the healthiest man in France, would not have been cut off in the flower of his age.

The Prince of Soubise, happy in the finest flush of health, would not have been snatched away at five-and-twenty, nor the Dauphin, grandfather to Louis XV., have been laid in his grave in his fiftieth year. Twenty thousand persons whom the small-pox swept away at Paris in 1723 would have been alive at this time. But are not the French fond of life, and is beauty so inconsiderable an advantage as to be disregarded by the ladies? It must be confessed that we are an odd kind of people. Perhaps our nation will imitate ten years hence this practice of the English, if the clergy and the physicians will but give them leave to do it; or possibly our countrymen may introduce inoculation three months hence in France out of mere whim, in case the English should discontinue it through fickleness.

Letters on the English; or Lettres Philosophiques

I am informed that the Chinese have practised inoculation these hundred years, a circumstance that argues very much in its favour, since they are thought to be the wisest and best governed people in the world. The Chinese, indeed, do not communicate this distemper by inoculation, but at the nose, in the same manner as we take snuff. This is a more agreeable way, but then it produces the like effects; and proves at the same time that had inoculation been practised in France it would have saved the lives of thousands.

Letter XII: On The Lord Bacon

Not long since the trite and frivolous question following was debated in a very polite and learned company, viz., Who was the greatest man, Caesar, Alexander, Tamerlane, Cromwell, &c.?

Somebody answered that Sir Isaac Newton excelled them all. The gentleman's assertion was very just; for if true greatness consists in having received from heaven a mighty genius, and in having employed it to enlighten our own mind and that of others, a man like Sir Isaac Newton, whose equal is hardly found in a thousand years, is the truly great man. And those politicians and conquerors (and all ages produce some) were generally so many illustrious wicked men. That man claims our respect who commands over the minds of the rest of the world by the force of truth, not those who enslave their fellow–creatures: he who is acquainted with the universe, not they who deface it.

Since, therefore, you desire me to give you an account of the famous personages whom England has given birth to, I shall begin with Lord Bacon, Mr. Locke, Sir Isaac Newton, &c. Afterwards the warriors and Ministers of State shall come in their order.

I must begin with the celebrated Viscount Verulam, known in Europe by the name of Bacon, which was that of his family. His father had been Lord Keeper, and himself was a great many years Lord Chancellor under King James I. Nevertheless, amidst the intrigues of a Court, and the affairs of his exalted employment, which alone were enough to engross his whole time, he yet found so much leisure for study as to make himself a great philosopher, a good historian, and an elegant writer; and a still more surprising circumstance is that he lived in an age in which the art of writing justly and elegantly was

Letters on the English; or Lettres Philosophiques

little known, much less true philosophy. Lord Bacon, as is the fate of man, was more esteemed after his death than in his lifetime. His enemies were in the British Court, and his admirers were foreigners.

When the Marquis d'Effiat attended in England upon the Princess Henrietta Maria, daughter to Henry IV., whom King Charles I, had married, that Minister went and visited the Lord Bacon, who, being at that time sick in his bed, received him with the curtains shut close. "You resemble the angels," said the Marquis to him; "we hear those beings spoken of perpetually, and we believe them superior to men, but are never allowed the consolation to see them."

You know that this great man was accused of a crime very unbecoming a philosopher: I mean bribery and extortion. You know that he was sentenced by the House of Lords to pay a fine of about four hundred thousand French livres, to lose his peerage and his dignity of Chancellor; but in the present age the English revere his memory to such a degree, that they will scarce allow him to have been guilty. In case you should ask what are my thoughts on this head, I shall answer you in the words which I heard the Lord Bolingbroke use on another occasion. Several gentlemen were speaking, in his company, of the avarice with which the late Duke of Marlborough had been charged, some examples whereof being given, the Lord Bolingbroke was appealed to (who, having been in the opposite party, might perhaps, without the imputation of indecency, have been allowed to clear up that matter): "He was so great a man," replied his lordship, "that I have forgot his vices."

I shall therefore confine myself to those things which so justly gained Lord Bacon the esteem of all Europe.

The most singular and the best of all his pieces is that which, at this time, is the most useless and the least read, I mean his Novum Scientiarum Organum. This is the scaffold with which the new philosophy was raised; and when the edifice was built, part of it at least, the scaffold was no longer of service.

The Lord Bacon was not yet acquainted with Nature, but then he knew, and pointed out, the several paths that lead to it. He had despised in his younger years the thing called philosophy in the Universities, and did all that lay in his power to prevent those societies of men instituted to improve human reason from depraving it by their quiddities, their

Letters on the English; or Lettres Philosophiques

horrors of the vacuum, their substantial forms, and all those impertinent terms which not only ignorance had rendered venerable, but which had been made sacred by their being rediculously blended with religion.

He is the father of experimental philosophy. It must, indeed, be confessed that very surprising secrets had been found out before his time–the sea–compass, printing, engraving on copper plates, oil–painting, looking–glasses; the art of restoring, in some measure, old men to their sight by spectacles; gunpowder, &c., had been discovered. A new world has been sought for, found, and conquered. Would not one suppose that these sublime discoveries had been made by the greatest philosophers, and in ages much more enlightened than the present? But it was far otherwise; all these great changes happened in the most stupid and barbarous times. Chance only gave birth to most of those inventions; and it is very probable that what is called chance contributed very much to the discovery of America; at least, it has been always thought that Christopher Columbus undertook his voyage merely on the relation of a captain of a ship which a storm had driven as far westward as the Caribbean Islands. Be this as it will, men had sailed round the world, and could destroy cities by an artificial thunder more dreadful than the real one; but, then, they were not acquainted with the circulation of the blood, the weight of the air, the laws of motion, light, the number of our planets, &c. And a man who maintained a thesis on Aristotle's "Categories," on the universals a part rei, or such–like nonsense, was looked upon as a prodigy.

The most astonishing, the most useful inventions, are not those which reflect the greatest honour on the human mind. It is to a mechanical instinct, which is found in many men, and not to true philosophy, that most arts owe their origin.

The discovery of fire, the art of making bread, of melting and preparing metals, of building houses, and the invention of the shuttle, are infinitely more beneficial to mankind than printing or the sea–compass: and yet these arts were invented by uncultivated, savage men.

What a prodigious use the Greeks and Romans made afterwards of mechanics! Nevertheless, they believed that there were crystal heavens, that the stars were small lamps which sometimes fell into the sea, and one of their greatest philosophers, after long researches, found that the stars were so many flints which had been detached from the earth.

Letters on the English; or Lettres Philosophiques

In a word, no one before the Lord Bacon was acquainted with experimental philosophy, nor with the several physical experiments which have been made since his time. Scarce one of them but is hinted at in his work, and he himself had made several. He made a kind of pneumatic engine, by which he guessed the elasticity of the air. He approached, on all sides as it were, to the discovery of its weight, and had very near attained it, but some time after Torricelli seized upon his truth. In a little time experimental philosophy began to be cultivated on a sudden in most parts of Europe. It was a hidden treasure which the Lord Bacon had some notion of, and which all the philosophers, encouraged by his promises, endeavoured to dig up.

But that which surprised me most was to read in his work, in express terms, the new attraction, the invention of which is ascribed to Sir Isaac Newton.

We must search, says Lord Bacon, whether there may not be a kind of magnetic power which operates between the earth and heavy bodies, between the moon and the ocean, between the planets, &c. In another place he says, either heavy bodies must be carried towards the centre of the earth, or must be reciprocally attracted by it; and in the latter case it is evident that the nearer bodies, in their falling, draw towards the earth, the stronger they will attract one another. We must, says he, make an experiment to see whether the same clock will of faster on the top of a mountain or at the bottom of a mine; whether the strength of the weights decreases on the mountain and increases in the mine. It is probable that the earth has a true attractive power.

This forerunner in philosophy was also an elegant writers, an historian, and a wit.

His moral essays are greatly esteemed, but they were drawn up in the view of instructing rather than of pleasing; and, as they are not a satire upon mankind, like Rochefoucauld's "Maxims," nor written upon a sceptical plan, Like Montaigne's "Essays," they are not so much read as those two ingenious authors.

His History of Henry VII. was looked upon as a masterpiece, but how is it possible that some persons can presume to compare so little a work with the history of our illustrious Thuanus?

Speaking about the famous impostor Perkin, son to a converted Jew, who assumed boldly the name and title of Richard IV., King of England, at the instigation of the Duchess of

Burgundy, and who disputed the crown with Henry VII., the Lord Bacon writes as follows:

"At this time the King began again to be haunted with sprites, by the magic and curious arts of the Lady Margaret, who raised up the ghost of Richard, Duke of York, second to King Edward IV., to walk and vex the King.

"After such time as she (Margaret of Burgundy) thought he (Perkin Warbeck) was perfect in his lesson, she began to cast with herself from what coast this blazing star should first appear, and at what time it must be upon the horizon of Ireland; for there had the like meteor strong influence before."

Methinks our sagacious Thuanus does not give in to such fustian, which formerly was looked upon as sublime, but in this age is justly called nonsense.

Letter XIII: On Mr. Locke

Perhaps no man ever had a more judicious or more methodical genius, or was a more acute logician than Mr. Locke, and yet he was not deeply skilled in the mathematics. This great man could never subject himself to the tedious fatigue of calculations, nor to the dry pursuit of mathematical truths, which do not at first present any sensible objects to the mind; and no one has given better proofs than he, that it is possible for a man to have a geometrical head without the assistance of geometry. Before his time, several great philosophers had declared, in the most positive terms, what the soul of man is; but as these absolutely knew nothing about it, they might very well be allowed to differ entirely in opinion from one another.

In Greece, the infant seat of arts and of errors, and where the grandeaur as well as folly of the human mind went such prodigious lenghts, the people used to reason about the soul in the very same manner as we do.

The divine Anaxagoras, in whose honour an altar was erected for his having taught mankind that the sun was greater than Peloponnesus, that snow was black, and that the

Letters on the English; or Lettres Philosophiques

heavens were of stone, affirmed that the soul was an aerial spirit, but at the same time immortal. Diogenes (not he who was a cynical philosopher after having coined base money) declared that the soul was a portion of the substance of God: an idea which we must confess was very sublime. Epicurus maintained that it was composed of parts in the same manner as the body.

Aristotle, who has been explained a thousand ways, because he is unintelligible, was of opinion, according to some of his disciples, that the understanding in all men is one and the same substance.

The divine Plato, master of the divine Aristotle,–and the divine Socrates, master of the divine Plato,–used to say that the soul was corporeal and eternal. No doubt but the demon of Socrates had instructed him in the nature of it. Some people, indeed, pretend that a man who boasted his being attended by a familiar genius must infallibly be either a knave or a madman, but this kind of people are seldom satisfied with anything but reason.

With regard to the Fathers of the Church, several in the primitive ages believed that the soul was human, and the angels and God corporeal. Men naturally improve upon every system. St. Bernard, as Father Mabillon confesses, taught that the soul after death does not see God in the celestial regions, but converses with Christ's human nature only. However, he was not believed this time on his bare word; the adventure of the crusade having a little sunk the credit of his oracles. Afterwards a thousand schoolmen arose, such as the Irrefragable Doctor, the Subtile Doctor, the Angelic Doctor, the Seraphic Doctor, and the Cherubic Doctor, who were all sure that they had a very clear and distinct idea of the soul, and yet wrote in such a manner, that one would conclude they were resolved no one should understand a word in their writings. Our Descartes, born to discover the errors of antiquity, and at the same time to substitute his own; and hurried away by that systematic spirit which throws a cloud over the minds of the greatest men, thought he had demonstrated that the soul is the same thing as thought, in the same manner as matter, in his opinion, is the same as extension. He asserted, that man thinks eternally, and that the soul, at its coming into the body, is informed with the whole series of metaphysical notions: knowing God, infinite space, possessing all abstract ideas–in a word, completely endued with the most sublime lights, which it unhappily forgets at its issuing from the womb.

Letters on the English; or Lettres Philosophiques

Father Malebranche, in his sublime illusions, not only admitted innate ideas, but did not doubt of our living wholly in God, and that God is, as it were, our soul.

Such a multitude of reasoners having written the romance of the soul, a sage at last arose, who gave, with an air of the greatest modesty, the history of it. Mr. Locke has displayed the human soul in the same manner as an excellent anatomist explains the springs of the human body. He everywhere takes the light of physics for his guide. He sometimes presumes to speak affirmatively, but then he presumes also to doubt. Instead of concluding at once what we know not, he examines gradually what we would know. He takes an infant at the instant of his birth; he traces, step by step, the progress of his understanding; examines what things he has in common with beasts, and what he possesses above them. Above all, he consults himself; the being conscious that he himself thinks.

"I shall leave," says he, "to those who know more of this matter than myself, the examining whether the soul exists before or after the organisation of our bodies. But I confess that it is my lot to be animated with one of those heavy souls which do not think always; and I am even so unhappy as not to conceive that it is more necessary the soul should think perpetually than that bodies should be for ever in motion."

With regard to myself, I shall boast that I have the honour to be as stupid in this particular as Mr. Locke. No one shall ever make me believe that I think always: and I am as little inclined as he could be to fancy that some weeks after I was conceived I was a very learned soul; knowing at that time a thousand things which I forgot at my birth; and possessing when in the womb (though to no manner of purpose) knowledge which I lost the instant I had occasion for it; and which I have never since been able to recover perfectly.

Mr. Locke, after having destroyed innate ideas; after having fully renounced the vanity of believing that we think always; after having laid down, from the most solid principles, that ideas enter the mind through the senses; having examined our simple and complex ideas; having traced the human mind through its several operations; having shown that all the languages in the world are imperfect, and the great abuse that is made of words every moment, he at last comes to consider the extent or rather the narrow limits of human knowledge. It was in this chapter he presumed to advance, but very modestly, the following words: "We shall, perhaps, never be capable of knowing whether a being,

Letters on the English; or Lettres Philosophiques

purely material, thinks or not." This sage assertion was, by more divines than one, looked upon as a scandalous declaration that the soul is material and mortal. Some Englishmen, devout after their way, sounded an alarm. The superstitious are the same in society as cowards in an army; they themselves are seized with a panic fear, and communicate it to others. It was loudly exclaimed that Mr. Locke intended to destroy religion; nevertheless, religion had nothing to do in the affair, it being a question purely philosophical, altogether independent of faith and revelation. Mr. Locke's opponents needed but to examine, calmly and impartially, whether the declaring that matter can think, implies a contradiction; and whether God is able to communicate thought to matter. But divines are too apt to begin their declarations with saying that God is offended when people differ from them in opinion; in which they too much resemble the bad poets, who used to declare publicly that Boileau spake irreverently of Louis XIV., because he ridiculed their stupid productions. Bishop Stillingfleet got the reputation of a calm and unprejudiced divine because he did not expressly make use of injurious terms in his dispute with Mr. Locke. That divine entered the lists against him, but was defeated; for he argued as a schoolman, and Locke as a philosopher, who was perfectly acquainted with the strong as well as the weak side of the human mind, and who fought with weapons whose temper he knew. If I might presume to give my opinion on so delicate a subject after Mr. Locke, I would say, that men have long disputed on the nature and the immortality of the soul. With regard to its immortality, it is impossible to give a demonstration of it, since its nature is still the subject of controversy; which, however, must be thoroughly understood before a person can be able to determine whether it be immortal or not. Human reason is so little able, merely by its own strength, to demonstrate the immortality of the soul, that it was absolutely necessary religion should reveal it to us. It is of advantage to society in general, that mankind should believe the soul to be immortal; faith commands us to do this; nothing more is required, and the matter is cleared up at once. But it is otherwise with respect to its nature; it is of little importance to religion, which only requires the soul to be virtuous, whatever substance it may be made of. It is a clock which is given us to regulate, but the artist has not told us of what materials the spring of this clock is composed.

I am a body, and, I think, that's all I know of the matter. Shall I ascribe to an unknown cause, what I can so easily impute to the only second cause I am acquainted with? Here all the school philosophers interrupt me with their arguments, and declare that there is only extension and solidity in bodies, and that there they can have nothing but motion and figure. Now motion, figure, extension and solidity cannot form a thought, and consequently the soul cannot be matter. All this so often repeated mighty series of reasoning, amounts to no more than this: I am absolutely ignorant what matter is; I guess, but imperfectly, some properties of it; now I absolutely cannot tell whether these properties may be joined to thought. As I therefore know nothing, I maintain positively that matter cannot think. In this manner do the schools reason.

Mr. Locke addressed these gentlemen in the candid, sincere manner following: At least confess yourselves to be as ignorant as I. Neither your imaginations nor mine are able to comprehend in what manner a body is susceptible of ideas; and do you conceive better in what manner a substance, of what kind soever, is susceptible of them? As you cannot comprehend either matter or spirit, why will you presume to assert anything?

The superstitious man comes afterwards and declares, that all those must be burnt for the good of their souls, who so much as suspect that it is possible for the body to think without any foreign assistance. But what would these people say should they themselves be proved irreligious? And indeed, what man can presume to assert, without being guilty at the same time of the greatest impiety, that it is impossible for the Creator to form matter with thought and sensation? Consider only, I beg you, what a dilemma you bring yourselves into, you who confine in this manner the power of the Creator. Beasts have the same organs, the same sensations, the same perceptions as we; they have memory, and combine certain ideas. In case it was not in the power of God to animate matter, and inform it with sensation, the consequence would be, either that beasts are mere machines, or that they have a spiritual soul.

Methinks it is clearly evident that beasts cannot be mere machines, which I prove thus. God has given to them the very same organs of sensation as to us: if therefore they have no sensation, God has created a useless thing; now according to your own confession God does nothing in vain; He therefore did not create so many organs of sensation, merely for them to be uninformed with this faculty; consequently beasts are not mere machines. Beasts, according to your assertion, cannot be animated with a spiritual soul; you will, therefore, in spite of yourself, be reduced to this only assertion, viz., that God has endued the organs of beasts, who are mere matter, with the faculties of sensation and perception, which you call instinct in them. But why may not God, if He pleases, communicate to our more delicate organs, that faculty of feeling, perceiving, and thinking, which we call human reason? To whatever side you turn, you are forced to acknowledge your own ignorance, and the boundless power of the Creator. Exclaim therefore no more against the sage, the modest philosophy of Mr. Locke, which so far from interfering with religion, would of be use to demonstrate the truth of it, in case religion wanted any such support. For what philosophy can be of a more religious nature than that, which affirming nothing but what it conceives clearly, and conscious of its own weakness, declares that we must always have recourse to God in our examining of the first principles?

Besides, we must not be apprehensive that any philosophical opinion will ever prejudice the religion of a country. Though our demonstrations clash directly with our mysteries, that is nothing to the purpose, for the latter are not less revered upon that account by our Christian philosophers, who know very well that the objects of reason and those of faith are of a very different nature. Philosophers will never form a religious sect, the reason of which is, their writings are not calculated for the vulgar, and they themselves are free from enthusiasm. If we divide mankind into twenty parts, it will be found that nineteen of these consist of persons employed in manual labour, who will never know that such a man as Mr. Locke existed. In the remaining twentieth part how few are readers? And among such as are so, twenty amuse themselves with romances to one who studies philosophy. The thinking part of mankind is confined to a very small number, and these will never disturb the peace and tranquillity of the world.

Neither Montaigne, Locke, Bayle, Spinoza, Hobbes, the Lord Shaftesbury, Collins, nor Toland lighted up the firebrand of discord in their countries; this has generally been the work of divines, who being at first puffed up with the ambition of becoming chiefs of a sect, soon grew very desirous of being at the head of a party. But what do I say? All the works of the modern philosophers put together will never make so much noise as even the dispute which arose among the Franciscans, merely about the fashion of their sleeves and of their cowls.

Letter XIV: On Descartes And Sir Isaac Newton

A Frenchman who arrives in London, will find philosophy, like everything else, very much changed there. He had left the world a plenum, and he now finds it a vacuum. At Paris the universe is seen composed of vortices of subtile matter; but nothing like it is

Letters on the English; or Lettres Philosophiques

seen in London. In France, it is the pressure of the moon that causes the tides; but in England it is the sea that gravitates towards the moon; so that when you think that the moon should make it flood with us, those gentlemen fancy it should be ebb, which very unluckily cannot be proved. For to be able to do this, it is necessary the moon and the tides should have been inquired into at the very instant of the creation.

You will observe farther, that the sun, which in France is said to have nothing to do in the affair, comes in here for very near a quarter of its assistance. According to your Cartesians, everything is performed by an impulsion, of which we have very little notion; and according to Sir Isaac Newton, it is by an attraction, the cause of which is as much unknown to us. At Paris you imagine that the earth is shaped like a melon, or of an oblique figure; at London it has an oblate one. A Cartesian declares that light exists in the air; but a Newtonian asserts that it comes from the sun in six minutes and a half. The several operations of your chemistry are performed by acids, alkalies and subtile matter; but attraction prevails even in chemistry among the English.

The very essence of things is totally changed. You neither are agreed upon the definition of the soul, nor on that of matter. Descartes, as I observed in my last, maintains that the soul is the same thing with thought, and Mr. Locke has given a pretty good proof of the contrary.

Descartes asserts farther, that extension alone constitutes matter, but Sir Isaac adds solidity to it.

How furiously contradictory are these opinions!

"Non nostrum inter vos tantas componere lites."

Virgil, Eclog. III.

"'Tis not for us to end such great disputes."

This famous Newton, this destroyer of the Cartesian system, died in March, anno 1727. His countrymen honoured him in his lifetime, and interred him as though he had been a king who had made his people happy.

Letters on the English; or Lettres Philosophiques

The English read with the highest satisfaction, and translated into their tongue, the Elogium of Sir Isaac Newton, which M. de Fontenelle spoke in the Academy of Sciences. M. de Fontenelle presides as judge over philosophers; and the English expected his decision, as a solemn declaration of the superiority of the English philosophy over that of the French. But when it was found that this gentleman had compared Descartes to Sir Isaac, the whole Royal Society in London rose up in arms. So far from acquiescing with M. Fontenelle's judgment, they criticised his discourse. And even several (who, however, were not the ablest philosophers in that body) were offended at the comparison, and for no other reason but because Descartes was a Frenchman.

It must be confessed that these two great men differed very much in conduct, in fortune, and in philosophy.

Nature had indulged Descartes with a shining and strong imagination, whence he became a very singular person both in private life and in his manner of reasoning. This imagination could not conceal itself even in his philosophical works, which are everywhere adorned with very shining, ingenious metaphors and figures. Nature had almost made him a poet; and indeed he wrote a piece of poetry for the entertainment of Christina, Queen of Sweden, which however was suppressed in honour to his memory.

He embraced a military life for some time, and afterwards becoming a complete philosopher, he did not think the passion of love derogatory to his character. He had by his mistress a daughter called Froncine, who died young, and was very much regretted by him. Thus the experienced every passion incident to mankind.

He was a long time of opinion that it would be necessary for him to fly from the society of his fellow creatures, and especially from his native country, in order to enjoy the happiness of cultivating his philosophical studies in full liberty.

Descartes was very right, for his contemporaries were not knowing enough to improve had enlighten his understanding, and were capable of little else than of giving him uneasiness.

He left France purely to go in search of truth, which was then persecuted by the wretched philosophy of the schools. However, he found that reason was as much disguised and depraved in the universities of Holland, into which he withdrew, as in his own country.

Letters on the English; or Lettres Philosophiques

For at the time that the French condemned the only propositions of his philosophy which were true, he was persecuted by the pretended philosophers of Holland, who understood him no better; and who, having a nearer view of his glory, hated his person the more, so that he was obliged to leave Utrecht. Descartes was injuriously accused of being an atheist, the last refuge of religious scandal: and he who had employed all the sagacity and penetration of his genius, in searching for new proofs of the existence of a God, was suspected to believe there was no such Being.

Such a persecution from all sides, must necessarily suppose a most exalted merit as well as a very distinguished reputation, and indeed he possessed both. Reason at that time darted a ray upon the world through the gloom of the schools, and the prejudices of popular superstition. At last his name spread so universally, that the French were desirous of bringing him back into his native country by rewards, and accordingly offered him an annual pension of a thousand crowns. Upon these hopes Descartes returned to France; paid the fees of his patent, which was sold at that time, but no pension was settled upon him. Thus disappointed, he returned to his solitude in North Holland, where he again pursued the study of philosophy, whilst the great Galileo, fourscore years of age, was groaning in the prisons of the Inquisition, only for having demonstrated the earth's motion.

At last Descartes was snatched from the world in the flower of his age at Stockholm. His death was owing to a bad regimen, and he expired in the midst of some literati who were his enemies, and under the hands of a physician to whom he was odious.

The progress of Sir Isaac Newton's life was quite different. He lived happy, and very much honoured in his native country, to the age of fourscore and five years.

It was his peculiar felicity, not only to be born in a country of liberty, but in an age when all scholastic impertinences were banished from the world. Reason alone was cultivated, and mankind could only be his pupil, not his enemy.

One very singular difference in the lives of these two great men is, that Sir Isaac, during the long course of years he enjoyed, was never sensible to any passion, was not subject to the common frailties of mankind, nor ever had any commerce with women–a circumstance which was assured me by the physician and surgeon who attended him in his last moments.

Letters on the English; or Lettres Philosophiques

We may admire Sir Isaac Newton on this occasion, but then we must not censure Descartes.

The opinion that generally prevails in England with regard to these new philosophers is, that the latter was a dreamer, and the former a sage.

Very few people in England read Descartes, whose works indeed are now useless. On the other side, but a small number peruse those of Sir Isaac, because to do this the student must be deeply skilled in the mathematics, otherwise those works will be unintelligible to him. But notwithstanding this, these great men are the subject of everyone's discourse. Sir Isaac Newton is allowed every advantage, whilst Descartes is not indulged a single one. According to some, it is to the former that we owe the discovery of a vacuum, that the air is a heavy body, and the invention of telescopes. In a word, Sir Isaac Newton is here as the Hercules of fabulous story, to whom the ignorant ascribed all the feats of ancient heroes.

In a critique that was made in London on M. de Fontenelle's discourse, the writer presumed to assert that Descartes was not a great geometrician. Those who make such a declaration may justly be reproached with flying in their master's face. Descartes extended the limits of geometry as far beyond the place where he found them, as Sir Isaac did after him. The former first taught the method of expressing curves by equations. This geometry which, thanks to him for it, is now grown common, was so abstruse in his time, that not so much as one professor would undertake to explain it; and Schotten in Holland, and Format in France, were the only men who understood it.

He applied this geometrical and inventive genius to dioptrics, which, when treated of by him, became a new art. And if he was mistaken in some things, the reason of that is, a man who discovers a new tract of land cannot at once know all the properties of the soil. Those who come after him, and make these lands fruitful, are at least obliged to him for the discovery. I will not deny but that there are innumerable errors in the rest of Descartes' works.

Geometry was a guide he himself had in some measure fashioned, which would have conducted him safely through the several paths of natural philosophy. Nevertheless, he at last abandoned this guide, and gave entirely into the humour of forming hypotheses; and then philosophy was no more than an ingenious romance, fit only to amuse the ignorant.

Letters on the English; or Lettres Philosophiques

He was mistaken in the nature of the soul, in the proofs of the existence of a God, in matter, in the laws of motion, and in the nature of light. He admitted innate ideas, he invented new elements, he created a world; he made man according to his own fancy; and it is justly said, that the man of Descartes is, in fact, that of Descartes only, very different from the real one.

He pushed his metaphysical errors so far, as to declare that two and two make four for no other reason by because God would have it so. However, it will not be making him too great a compliment if we affirm that he was valuable even in his mistakes. He deceived himself, but then it was at least in a methodical way. He destroyed all the absurd chimeras with which youth had been infatuated for two thousand years. He taught his contemporaries how to reason, and enabled them to employ his own weapons against himself. If Descartes did not pay in good money, he however did great service in crying down that of a base alloy.

I indeed believe that very few will presume to compare his philosophy in any respect with that of Sir Isaac Newton. The former is an essay, the latter a masterpiece. But then the man who first brought us to the path of truth, was perhaps as great a genius as he who afterwards conducted us through it.

Descartes gave sight to the blind. These saw the errors of antiquity and of the sciences. The path he struck out is since become boundless. Robault's little work was, during some years, a complete system of physics; but now all the Transactions of the several academies in Europe put together do not form so much as the beginning of a system. In fathoming this abyss no bottom has been found. We are now to examine what discoveries Sir Isaac Newton has made in it.

Letter XV: On Attraction

The discoveries which gained Sir Isaac Newton so universal a reputation, relate to the system of the world, to light, to geometrical infinities; and, lastly, to chronology, with which he used to amuse himself after the fatigue of his severer studies.

Letters on the English; or Lettres Philosophiques

I will now acquaint you (without prolixity if possible) with the few things I have been able to comprehend of all these sublime ideas. With regard to the system of our world disputes were a long time maintained, on the cause that turns the planets, and keeps them in their orbits; and on those causes which make all bodies here below descend towards the surface of the earth.

The system of Descartes, explained and improved since his time, seemed to give a plausible reason for all those phenomena; and this reason seemed more just, as it is simple and intelligible to all capacities. But in philosophy, a student ought to doubt of the things he fancies he understands too easily, as much as of those he does not understand.

Gravity, the falling of accelerated bodies on the earth, the revolution of the planets in their orbits, their rotations round their axis, all this is mere motion. Now motion cannot perhaps be conceived any otherwise than by impulsion; therefore all those bodies must be impelled. But by what are they impelled? All space is full, it therefore is filled with a very subtle matter, since this is imperceptible to us; this matter goes from west to east, since all the planets are carried from west to east. Thus from hypothesis to hypothesis, from one appearance to another, philosophers have imagined a vast whirlpool of subtle matter, in which the planets are carried round the sun: they also have created another particular vortex which floats in the great one, and which turns daily round the planets. When all this is done, it is pretended that gravity depends on this diurnal motion; for, say these, the velocity of the subtle matter that turns round our little vortex, must be seventeen times more rapid than that of the earth; or, in case its velocity is seventeen times greater than that of the earth, its centrifugal force must be vastly greater, and consequently impel all bodies towards the earth. This is the cause of gravity, according to the Cartesian system. But the theorist, before he calculated the centrifugal force and velocity of the subtle matter, should first have been certain that it existed.

Sir Isaac Newton seems to have destroyed all these great and little vortices, both that which carries the planets round the sun, as well as the other which supposes every planet to turn on its own axis.

First, with regard to the pretended little vortex of the earth, it is demonstrated that it must lose its motion by insensible degrees; it is demonstrated, that if the earth swims in a fluid, its density must be equal to that of the earth; and in case its density be the same, all the bodies we endeavour to move must meet with an insuperable resistance.

Letters on the English; or Lettres Philosophiques

With regard to the great vortices, they are still more chimerical, and it is impossible to make them agree with Kepler's law, the truth of which has been demonstrated. Sir Isaac shows, that the revolution of the fluid in which Jupiter is supposed to be carried, is not the same with regard to the revolution of the fluid of the earth, as the revolution of Jupiter with respect to that of the earth. He proves, that as the planets make their revolutions in ellipses, and consequently being at a much greater distance one from the other in their Aphelia, and a little nearer in their Perihelia; the earth's velocity, for instance, ought to be greater when it is nearer Venus and Mars, because the fluid that carries it along, being then more pressed, ought to have a greater motion; and yet it is even then that the earth's motion is slower.

He proves that there is no such thing as a celestial matter which goes from west to east since the comets traverse those spaces, sometimes from east to west, and at other times from north to south.

In fine, the better to resolve, if possible, every difficulty, he proves, and even by experiments, that it is impossible there should be a plenum; and brings back the vacuum, which Aristotle and Descartes had banished from the world.

Having by these and several other arguments destroyed the Cartesian vortices, he despaired of ever being able to discover whether there is a secret principle in nature which, at the same time, is the cause of the motion of all celestial bodies, and that of gravity on the earth. But being retired in 1666, upon account of the Plague, to a solitude near Cambridge; as he was walking one day in his garden, and saw some fruits fall from a tree, he fell into a profound meditation on that gravity, the cause of which had so long been sought, but in vain, by all the philosophers, whilst the vulgar think there is nothing mysterious in it. He said to himself, that from what height soever in our hemisphere, those bodies might descend, their fall would certainly be in the progression discovered by Galileo; and the spaces they run through would be as the square of the times. Why may not this power which causes heavy bodies to descend, and is the same without any sensible diminution at the remotest distance from the centre of the earth, or on the summits of the highest mountains, why, said Sir Isaac, may not this power extend as high as the moon? And in case its influence reaches so far, is it not very probable that this power retains it in its orbit, and determines its motion? But in case the moon obeys this principle (whatever it be) may we not conclude very naturally that the rest of the planets are equally subject to it? In case this power exists (which besides is proved) it must increase in an inverse ratio of the squares of the distances. All, therefore, that remains is, to examine how far a heavy body, which should fall upon the earth from a moderate height, would go; and how far in the same time, a body which should fall from the orbit of the moon, would descend. To find this, nothing is wanted but the measure of the earth, and the distance of the moon from it.

Thus Sir Isaac Newton reasoned. But at that time the English had but a very imperfect measure of our globe, and depended on the uncertain supposition of mariners, who computed a degree to contain but sixty English miles, whereas it consists in reality of near seventy. As this false computation did not agree with the conclusions which Sir Isaac intended to draw from them, he laid aside this pursuit. A half-learned philosopher, remarkable only for his vanity, would have made the measure of the earth agree, anyhow, with his system. Sir Isaac, however, chose rather to quit the researches he was then engaged in. But after Mr. Picard had measured the earth exactly, by tracing that meridian which redounds so much to the honour of the French, Sir Isaac Newton resumed is former reflections, and found his account in Mr. Picard's calculation.

A circumstance which has always appeared wonderful to me, is that such sublime discoveries should have been made by the sole assistance of a quadrant and a little arithmetic.

The circumference of the earth is 123,249,600 feet. This, among other things, is necessary to prove the system of attraction.

The instant we know the earth's circumference, and the distance of the moon, we know that of the moon's orbit, and the diameter of this orbit. The moon performs its revolution in that orbit in twenty-seven days, seven hours, forty-three minutes. It is demonstrated, that the moon in its mean motion makes an hundred and fourscore and seven thousand nine hundred and sixty feet (of Paris) in a minute. It is likewise demonstrated, by a known theorem, that the central force which should make a body fall from the height of the moon, would make its velocity no more than fifteen Paris feet in a minute of time. Now if the law by which bodies gravitate and attract one another in an inverse ratio to the squares of the distances be true, if the same power acts according to that law throughout all nature, it is evident that as the earth is sixty semi-diameters distant from the moon, a heavy body must necessarily fall (on the earth) fifteen feet in the first second, and fifty-four thousand feet in the first minute.

Letters on the English; or Lettres Philosophiques

Now a heavy body falls, in reality, fifteen feet in the first second, and goes in the first minute fifty-four thousand feet, which number is the square of sixty multiplied by fifteen. Bodies, therefore, gravitate in an inverse ratio of the squares of the distances; consequently, what causes gravity on earth, and keeps the moon in its orbit, is one and the same power; it being demonstrated that the moon gravitates on the earth, which is the centre of its particular motion, it is demonstrated that the earth and the moon gravitate on the sun which is the centre of their annual motion.

The rest of the planets must be subject to this general law; and if this law exists, these planets must follow the laws which Kepler discovered. All these laws, all these relations are indeed observed by the planets with the utmost exactness; therefore, the power of attraction causes all the planets to gravitate towards the sun, in like manner as the moon gravitates towards our globe.

Finally as in all bodies re-action is equal to action, it is certain that the earth gravitates also towards the moon; and that the sun gravitates towards both. That every one of the satellites of Saturn gravitates towards the other four, and the other four towards it; all five towards Saturn, and Saturn towards all. That it is the same with regard to Jupiter; and that all these globes are attracted by the sun, which is reciprocally attracted by them.

This power of gravitation acts proportionably to the quantity of matter in bodies, a truth, which Sir Isaac has demonstrated by experiments. This new discovery has been of use to show that the sun (the centre of the planetary system) attracts them all in a direct ratio of their quantity of matter combined with their nearness. From hence Sir Isaac, rising by degrees to discoveries which seemed not to be formed for the human mind, is bold enough to compute the quantity of matter contained in the sun and in every planet; and in this manner shows, from the simple laws of mechanics, that every celestial globe ought necessarily to be where it is placed.

His bare principle of the laws of gravitation accounts for all the apparent inequalities in the course of the celestial globes. The variations of the moon are a necessary consequence of those laws. Moreover, the reason is evidently seen why the nodes of the moon perform their revolutions in nineteen years, and those of the earth in about twenty-six thousand. The several appearances observed in the tides are also a very simple effect of this attraction. The proximity of the moon, when at the full, and when it is new, and its distance in the quadratures or quarters, combined with the action of the sun, exhibit a sensible reason why the ocean swells and sinks.

After having shown by his sublime theory the course and inequalities of the planets, he subjects comets to the same law. The orbit of these fires (unknown for so great a series of years), which was the terror of mankind and the rock against which philosophy split, placed by Aristotle below the moon, and sent back by Descartes above the sphere of Saturn, is at last placed in its proper seat by Sir Isaac Newton.

He proves that comets are solid bodies which move in the sphere of the sun's activity, and that they describe an ellipsis so very eccentric, and so near to parabolas, that certain comets must take up above five hundred years in their revolution.

The learned Dr. Halley is of opinion that the comet seen in 1680 is the same which appeared in Julius Caesar's time. This shows more than any other that comets are hard, opaque bodies; for it descended so near to the sun, as to come within a sixth part of the diameter of this planet from it, and consequently might have contracted a degree of heat two thousand times stronger than that of red-hot iron; and would have been soon dispersed in vapour, had it not been a firm, dense body. The guessing the course of comets began then to be very much in vogue. The celebrated Bernoulli concluded by his system than the famous comet of 1680 would appear again the 17th of May, 1719. Not a single astronomer in Europe went to bed that night. However, they needed not to have broke their rest, for the famous comet never appeared. There is at least more cunning, if not more certainty, in fixing its return to so remote a distance as five hundred and seventy-five years. As to Mr. Whiston, he affirmed very seriously that in the time of the Deluge a comet overflowed the terrestrial globe. And he was so unreasonable as to wonder that people laughed at him for making such an assertion. The ancients were almost in the same way of thinking with Mr. Whiston, and fancied that comets were always the forerunners of some great calamity which was to befall mankind. Sir Isaac Newton, on the contrary, suspected that they are very beneficent, and that vapours exhale from them merely to nourish and vivify the planets, which imbibe in their course the several particles the sun has detached from the comets, an opinion which, at least, is more probable than the former. But this is not all. If this power of gravitation or attraction acts on all the celestial globes, it acts undoubtedly on the several parts of these globes. For in case bodies attract one another in proportion to the quantity of matter contained in them, it can only be in proportion to the quantity of their parts; and if this power is found in the whole, it is undoubtedly in the half, in the quarter, in the eighth part, and so on in

Letters on the English; or Lettres Philosophiques

infinitum.

This is attraction, the great spring by which all Nature is moved. Sir Isaac Newton, after having demonstrated the existence of this principle, plainly foresaw that its very name would offend; and, therefore, this philosopher, in more places than one of his books, gives the reader some caution about it. He bids him beware of confounding this name with what the ancients called occult qualities, but to be satisfied with knowing that there is in all bodies a central force, which acts to the utmost limits of the universe, according to the invariable laws of mechanics.

It is surprising, after the solemn protestations Sir Isaac made, that such eminent men as Mr. Sorin and M. de Fontenelle should have imputed to this great philosopher the verbal and chimerical way of reasoning of the Aristotelians; Mr. Sorin in the Memoirs of the Academy of 1709, and M. de Fontenelle in the very eulogium of Sir Isaac Newton.

Most of the French (the learned and others) have repeated this reproach. These are for ever crying out, "Why did he not employ the word impulsion, which is so well understood, rather than that of attraction, which is unintelligible?"

Sir Isaac might have answered these critics thus:–"First, you have as imperfect an idea of the word impulsion as of that of attraction; and in case you cannot conceive how one body tends towards the centre of another body, neither can you conceive by what power one body can impel another.

"Secondly, I could not admit of impulsion; for to do this I must have known that a celestial matter was the agent. But so far from knowing that there is any such matter, I have proved it to be merely imaginary.

"Thirdly, I use the word attraction for no other reason but to express an effect which I discovered in Nature–a certain and indisputable effect of an unknown principle–a quality inherent in matter, the cause of which persons of greater abilities that I can pretend to may, if they can, find out."

"What have you, then, taught us?" will these people say further; "and to what purpose are so many calculations to tell us what you yourself do not comprehend?"

Letters on the English; or Lettres Philosophiques

"I have taught you," may Sir Isaac rejoin, "that all bodies gravitate towards one another in proportion to their quantity of matter; that these central forces alone keep the planets and comets in their orbits, and cause them to move in the proportion before set down. I demonstrate to you that it is impossible there should be any other cause which keeps the planets in their orbits than that general phenomenon of gravity. For heavy bodies fall on the earth according to the proportion demonstrated of central forces; and the planets finishing their course according to these same proportions, in case there were another power that acted upon all those bodies, it would either increase their velocity or change their direction. Now, not one of those bodies ever has a single degree of motion or velocity, or has any direction but what is demonstrated to be the effect of the central forces. Consequently it is impossible there should be any other principle."

Give me leave once more to introduce Sir Isaac speaking. Shall he not be allowed to say, "My case and that of the ancients is very different. These saw, for instance, water ascend in pumps, and said, 'the water rises because it abhors a vacuum.' But with regard to myself, I am in the case of a man who should have first observed that water ascends in pumps, but should leave others to explain the cause of this effect. The anatomist, who first declared that the motion of the arm is owing to the contraction of the muscles, taught mankind an indisputable truth. But are they less obliged to him because he did not know the reason why the muscles contract? The cause of the elasticity of the air is unknown, but he who first discovered this spring performed a very signal service to natural philosophy. The spring that I discovered was more hidden and more universal, and for that very reason mankind ought to thank me the more. I have discovered a new property of matter–one of the secrets of the Creator–and have calculated and discovered the effects of it. After this, shall people quarrel with me about the name I give it?"

Vortices may be called an occult quality because their existence was never proved. Attraction, on the contrary, is a real thing because its effects are demonstrated, and the proportions of it are calculated. The cause of this cause is among the Arcana of the Almighty.

"Procedes huc, et non amplius."

(Thus far shalt thou go, and no farther.)

Letters on the English; or Lettres Philosophiques

Letter XVI: On Sir Isaac Newton's Optics

The philosophers of the last age found out a new universe; and a circumstance which made its discovery more difficult was that no one had so much as suspected its existence. The most sage and judicious were of opinion that it was a frantic rashness to dare so much as to imagine that it was possible to guess the laws by which the celestial bodies move and the manner how light acts. Galileo, by his astronomical discoveries, Kepler, by his calculation, Descartes (at least, in his dioptrics), and Sir Isaac Newton, in all his works, severally saw the mechanism of the springs of the world. The geometricians have subjected infinity to the laws of calculation. The circulation of the blood in animals, and of the sap in vegetables, have changed the face of Nature with regard to us. A new kind of existence has been given to bodies in the air–pump. By the assistance of telescopes bodies have been brought nearer to one another. Finally, the several discoveries which Sir Isaac Newton has made on light are equal to the boldest things which the curiosity of man could expect after so many philosophical novelties.

Till Antonio de Dominis the rainbow was considered as an inexplicable miracle. This philosopher guessed that it was a necessary effect of the sun and rain. Descartes gained immortal fame by his mathematical explication of this so natural a phenomenon. He calculated the reflections and refractions of light in drops of rain. And his sagacity on this occasion was at that time looked upon as next to divine.

But what would he have said had it been proved to him that he was mistaken in the nature of light; that he had not the least reason to maintain that it is a globular body? That it is false to assert that this matter, spreading itself through the whole, waits only to be projected forward by the sun, in order to be put in action, in like manner as a long staff acts at one end when pushed forward by the other. That light is certainly darted by the sun; in fine, that light is transmitted from the sun to the earth in about seven minutes through a cannon–ball, which were not to lose any of its velocity, could not go that distance in less than twenty–five years. How great would have been his astonishment had he been told that light does not reflect directly by impinging against the solid parts of bodies, that bodies are not transparent when they have large pores, and that a man should arise who would demonstrate all these paradoxes, and anatomise a single ray of light with more dexterity than the ablest artist dissects a human body. This man is come. Sir Isaac Newton has demonstrated to the eye, by the bare assistance of the prism, that light is a composition of coloured rays, which, being united, form white colour. A single ray is by him divided into seven, which all fall upon a piece of linen, or a sheet of white paper, in their order, one above the other, and at unequal distances. The first is red, the second orange, the third yellow, the fourth green, the fifth blue, the sixth indigo, the seventh a violet–purple. Each of these rays, transmitted afterwards by a hundred other prisms, will never change the colour it bears; in like manner, as gold, when completely purged from its dross, will never change afterwards in the crucible. As a superabundant proof that each of these elementary rays has inherently in itself that which forms its colour to the eye, take a small piece of yellow wood, for instance, and set it in the ray of a red colour; this wood will instantly be tinged red. But set it in the ray of a green colour, it assumes a green colour, and so of all the rest.

From what cause, therefore, do colours arise in Nature? It is nothing but the disposition of bodies to reflect the rays of a certain order and to absorb all the rest.

What, then, is this secret disposition? Sir Isaac Newton demonstrates that it is nothing more than the density of the small constituent particles of which a body is composed. And how is this reflection performed? It was supposed to arise from the rebounding of the rays, in the same manner as a ball on the surface of a solid body. But this is a mistake, for Sir Isaac taught the astonished philosophers that bodies are opaque for no other reason but because their pores are large, that light reflects on our eyes from the very bosom of those pores, that the smaller the pores of a body are the more such a body is transparent. Thus paper, which reflects the light when dry, transmits it when oiled, because the oil, by filling its pores, makes them much smaller.

It is there that examining the vast porosity of bodies, every particle having its pores, and every particle of those particles having its own, he shows we are not certain that there is a cubic inch of solid matter in the universe, so far are we from conceiving what matter is. Having thus divided, as it were, light into its elements, and carried the sagacity of his discoveries so far as to prove the method of distinguishing compound colours from such as are primitive, he shows that these elementary rays, separated by the prism, are ranged in their order for no other reason but because they are refracted in that very order; and it is this property (unknown till he discovered it) of breaking or splitting in this proportion; it is this unequal refraction of rays, this power of refracting the red less than the orange colour, &c., which he calls the different refrangibility. The most reflexible rays are the most refrangible, and from hence he evinces that the same power is the cause both of the reflection and refraction of light.

But all these wonders are merely but the opening of his discoveries. He found out the secret to see the vibrations or fits of light which come and go incessantly, and which either transmit light or reflect it, according to the density of the parts they meet with. He has presumed to calculate the density of the particles of air necessary between two glasses, the one flat, the other convex on one side, set one upon the other, in order to operate such a transmission or reflection, or to form such and such a colour.

From all these combinations he discovers the proportion in which light acts on bodies and bodies act on light.

He saw light so perfectly, that he has determined to what degree of perfection the art of increasing it, and of assisting our eyes by telescopes, can be carried.

Descartes, from a noble confidence that was very excusable, considering how strongly he was fired at the first discoveries he made in an art which he almost first found out; Descartes, I say, hoped to discover in the stars, by the assistance of telescopes, objects as small as those we discern upon the earth.

But Sir Isaac has shown that dioptric telescopes cannot be brought to a greater perfection, because of that refraction, and of that very refrangibility, which at the same time that they bring objects nearer to us, scatter too much the elementary rays. He has calculated in these glasses the proportion of the scattering of the red and of the blue rays; and proceeding so far as to demonstrate things which were not supposed even to exist, he examines the inequalities which arise from the shape or figure of the glass, and that which arises from the refrangibility. He finds that the object glass of the telescope being convex on one side and flat on the other, in case the flat side be turned towards the object, the error which arises from the construction and position of the glass is above five thousand times less than the error which arises from the refrangibility; and, therefore, that the shape or figure of the glasses is not the cause why telescopes cannot be carried to a greater perfection, but arises wholly from the nature of light.

For this reason he invented a telescope, which discovers objects by reflection, and not by refraction. Telescopes of this new kind are very hard to make, and their use is not easy; but, according to the English, a reflective telescope of but five feet has the same effect as another of a hundred feet in length.

Letter XVII: On Infinites In Geometry, And Sir Isaac Newton's Chronology

The labyrinth and abyss of infinity is also a new course Sir Isaac Newton has gone through, and we are obliged to him for the clue, by whose assistance we are enabled to trace its various windings.

Descartes got the start of him also in this astonishing invention. He advanced with mighty steps in his geometry, and was arrived at the very borders of infinity, but went not farther. Dr. Wallis, about the middle of the last century, was the first who reduced a fraction by a perpetual division to an infinite series.

The Lord Brouncker employed this series to square the hyperbola. Mercator published a demonstration of this quadrature; much about which time Sir Isaac Newton, being then twenty-three years of age, had invented a general method, to perform on all geometrical curves what had just before been tried on the hyperbola.

It is to this method of subjecting everywhere infinity to algebraical calculations, that the name is given of differential calculations or of fluxions and integral calculation. It is the art of numbering and measuring exactly a thing whose existence cannot be conceived.

And, indeed, would you not imagine that a man laughed at you who should declare that there are lines infinitely great which form an angle infinitely little?

That a right line, which is a right line so long as it is finite, by changing infinitely little its direction, becomes an infinite curve; and that a curve may become infinitely less than another curve?

That there are infinite squares, infinite cubes, and infinites of infinites, all greater than one another, and the last but one of which is nothing in comparison of the last?

Letters on the English; or Lettres Philosophiques

All these things, which at first appear to be the utmost excess of frenzy, are in reality an effort of the sublety and extent of the human mind, and the art of finding truths which till then had been unknown.

This so bold edifice is even founded on simple ideas. The business is to measure the diagonal of a square, to give the area of a curve, to find the square root of a number, which has none in common arithmetic. After all, the imagination ought not to be startled any more at so many orders of infinites than at the so well-known proposition, viz., that curve lines may always be made to pass between a circle and a tangent, or at that other, namely, that matter is divisible in infinitum. These two truths have been demonstrated many years, and are no less incomprehensible than the things we have been speaking of.

For many years the invention of this famous calculation was denied to Sir Isaac Newton. In Germany Mr. Leibnitz was considered as the inventor of the differences or moments, called fluxions, and Mr. Bernoulli claimed the integral calculus. However, Sir Isaac is now thought to have first made the discovery, and the other two have the glory of having once made the world doubt whether it was to be ascribed to him or them. Thus some contested with Dr. Harvey the invention of the circulation of the blood, as others disputed with Mr. Perrault that of the circulation of the sap.

Hartsocher and Leuwenhoek disputed with each other the honour of having first seen the vermiculi of which mankind are formed. This Hartsocher also contested with Huygens the invention of a new method of calculating the distance of a fixed star. It is not yet known to what philosopher we owe the invention of the cycloid.

Be this as it will, it is by the help of this geometry of infinites that Sir Isaac Newton attained to the most sublime discoveries. I am now to speak of another work, which, though more adapted to the capacity of the human mind, does nevertheless display some marks of that creative genius with which Sir Isaac Newton was informed in all his researches. The work I mean is a chronology of a new kind, for what province soever he undertook he was sure to change the ideas and opinions received by the rest of men.

Accustomed to unravel and disentangle chaos, he was resolved to convey at least some light into that of the fables of antiquity which are blended and confounded with history, and fix an uncertain chronology. It is true that there is no family, city, or nation, but endeavours to remove its original as far backward as possible. Besides, the first historians were the most negligent in setting down the eras: books were infinitely less common than they are at this time, and, consequently, authors being not so obnoxious to censure, they therefore imposed upon the world with greater impunity; and, as it is evident that these have related a great number of fictitious particulars, it is probable enough that they also gave us several false eras.

It appeared in general to Sir Isaac that the world was five hundred years younger than chronologers declare it to be. He grounds his opinion on the ordinary course of Nature, and on the observations which astronomers have made.

By the course of Nature we here understand the time that every generation of men lives upon the earth. The Egyptians first employed this vague and uncertain method of calculating when they began to write the beginning of their history. These computed three hundred and forty-one generations from Menes to Sethon; and, having no fixed era, they supposed three generations to consist of a hundred years. In this manner they computed eleven thousand three hundred and forty years from Menes' reign to that of Sethon.

The Greeks before they counted by Olympiads followed the method of the Egyptians, and even gave a little more extent to generations, making each to consist of forty years.

Now, here, both the Egyptians and the Greeks made an errenous computation. It is true, indeed, that, according to the usual course of Nature, three generations last about a hundred and twenty years; but three reigns are far from taking up so many. It is very evident that mankind in general live longer than kings are found to reign, so that an author who should write a history in which there were no dates fixed, and should know that nine kings had reigned over a nation; such a historian would commit a great error should he allow three hundred years to these nine monarchs. Every generation takes about thirty-six years; every reign is, one with the other, about twenty. Thirty kings of England have swayed the sceptre from William the Conqueror to George I., the years of whose reigns added together amount to six hundred and forty-eight years; which, being divided equally among the thirty kings, give to every one a reign of twenty-one years and a half very near. Sixty-three kings of France have sat upon the throne; these have, one with another, reigned about twenty years each. This is the usual course of Nature. The ancients, therefore, were mistaken when they supposed the durations in general of reigns to equal that of generations. They, therefore, allowed too great a number of years, and consequently some years must be subtracted from their computation.

Letters on the English; or Lettres Philosophiques

Astronomical observations seem to have lent a still greater assistance to our philosopher. He appears to us stronger when he fights upon his own ground.

You know that the earth, besides its annual motion which carries it round the sun from west to east in the space of a year, has also a singular revolution which was quite unknown till within these late years. Its poles have a very slow retrograde motion from east to west, whence it happens that their position every day does not correspond exactly with the same point of the heavens. This difference which is so insensible in a year, becomes pretty considerable in time; and in threescore and twelve years the difference is found to be of one degree, that is to say, the three hundred and sixtieth part of the circumference of the whole heaven. Thus after seventy-two years the colure of the vernal equinox which passed through a fixed star, corresponds with another fixed star. Hence it is that the sun, instead of being in that part of the heavens in which the Ram was situated in the time of Hipparchus, is found to correspond with that part of the heavens in which the Bull was situated; and the Twins are placed where the Bull then stood. All the signs have changed their situation, and yet we still retain the same manner of speaking as the ancients did. In this age we say that the sun is in the Ram in the spring, from the principle of condescension that we say that the sun turns round.

Hipparchus was the first among the Greeks who observed some change in the constellations with regard to the equinoxes, or rather who learnt it from the Egyptians. Philosophers ascribed this motion to the stars; for in those ages people were far from imagining such a revolution in the earth, which was supposed to be immovable in every respect. They therefore created a heaven in which they fixed the several stars, and gave this heaven a particular motion by which it was carried towards the east, whilst that all the stars seemed to perform their diurnal revolution from east to west. To this error they added a second of much greater consequence, by imagining that the pretended heaven of the fixed stars advanced one degree eastward every hundred years. In this manner they were no less mistaken in their astronomical calculation than in their system of natural philosophy. As for instance, an astronomer in that age would have said that the vernal equinox was in the time of such and such an observation, in such a sign, and in such a star. It has advanced two degrees of each since the time that observation was made to the present. Now two degrees are equivalent to two hundred years; consequently the astronomer who made that observation lived just so many years before me. It is certain that an astronomer who had argued in this manner would have mistook just fifty-four years; hence it is that the ancients, who were doubly deceived, made their great year of the world, that is, the revolution of the whole heavens, to consist of thirty-six thousand years. But the moderns are sensible that this imaginary revolution of the heaven of the stars is nothing else than the revolution of the poles of the earth, which is performed in twenty-five thousand nine hundred years. It may be proper to observe transiently in this place, that Sir Isaac, by determining the figure of the earth, has very happily explained the cause of this revolution.

All this being laid down, the only thing remaining to settle chronology is to see through what star the colure of the equinoxes passes, and where it intersects at this time the ecliptic in the spring; and to discover whether some ancient writer does not tell us in what point the ecliptic was intersected in his time, by the same colure of the equinoxes.

Clemens Alexandrinus informs us, that Chiron, who went with the Argonauts, observed the constellations at the time of that famous expedition, and fixed the vernal equinox to the middle of the Ram; the autumnal equinox to the middle of Libra; our summer solstice to the middle of Cancer, and our winter solstice to the middle of Capricorn.

A long time after the expedition of the Argonauts, and a year before the Peloponnesian war, Methon observed that the point of the summer solstice passed through the eighth degree of Cancer.

Now every sign of the zodiac contains thirty degrees. In Chiron's time, the solstice was arrived at the middle of the sign, that is to say to the fifteenth degree. A year before the Peloponnesian war it was at the eighth, and therefore it had retarded seven degrees. A degree is equivalent to seventy-two years; consequently, from the beginning of the Peloponnesian war to the expedition of the Argonauts, there is no more than an interval of seven times seventy-two years, which make five hundred and four years, and not seven hundred years, as the Greeks computed. Thus in comparing the position of the heavens at this time with their position in that age, we find that the expedition of the Argonauts ought to be placed about nine hundred years before Christ, and not about fourteen hundred; and consequently that the world is not so old by five hundred years as it was generally supposed to be. By this calculation all the eras are drawn nearer, and the several events are found to have happened later than is computed. I don't know whether this ingenious system will be favourably received; and whether these notions will prevail so far with the learned, as to prompt them to reform the chronology of the world. Perhaps these gentlemen would think it too great a condescension to allow one and the same man the glory of having improved natural philosophy, geometry, and history. This would be a kind of universal monarchy, with which the principle of self-love that is in man will scarce suffer him to indulge his fellow-creature; and, indeed, at the same time that some very great philosophers attacked Sir Isaac Newton's attractive principle, others fell upon his chronological system. Time, that should discover to which of these the victory is due, may perhaps only leave the dispute still more undetermined.

Letter XVIII: On Tragedy

The English as well as the Spaniards were possessed of theatres at a time when the French had no more than moving, itinerant stages. Shakspeare, who was considered as the Corneille of the first-mentioned nation, was pretty nearly contemporary with Lope de Vega, and he created, as it were, the English theatre. Shakspeare boasted a strong fruitful genius. He was natural and sublime, but had not so much as a single spark of good taste, or knew one rule of the drama. I will now hazard a random, but, at the same time, true reflection, which is, that the great merit of this dramatic poet has been the ruin of the English stage. There are such beautiful, such noble, such dreadful scenes in this writer's monstrous farces, to which the name of tragedy is given, that they have always been exhibited with great success. Time, which alone gives reputation to writers, at last makes their very faults venerable. Most of the whimsical gigantic images of this poet, have, through length of time (it being a hundred and fifty years since they were first drawn) acquired a right of passing for sublime. Most of the modern dramatic writers have copied him: but the touches and descriptions which are applauded in Shakspeare. are hissed at in these writers; and you will easily believe that the veneration in which this author is held, increases in proportion to the contempt which is shown to the moderns. Dramatic writers don't consider that they should not imitate him; and the ill-success of Shakspeare's imitators produces no other effect, than to make him be considered as inimitable. You remember that in the tragedy of Othello, Moor of Venice, a most tender piece, a man strangles his wife on the stage; and that the poor woman, whilst she is strangling, cries aloud that she dies very unjustly. You know that in Hamlet, Prince of Denmark, two grave-diggers make a grave, and are all the time drinking, singing ballads, and making humorous reflections (natural indeed enough to persons of their profession) on the several skulls they throw up with their spades; but a circumstance which will surprise you is, that

Letters on the English; or Lettres Philosophiques

this ridiculous incident has been imitated. In the reign of King Charles II., which was that of politeness, and the Golden Age of the liberal arts; Otway, in his Venice Preserved, introduces Antonio the senator, and Naki, his courtesan, in the midst of the horrors of the Marquis of Bedemar's conspiracy. Antonio, the super-annuated senator plays, in his mistress' presence, all the apish tricks of a lewd, impotent debauchee, who is quite frantic and out of his senses. He mimics a bull and a dog, and bites his mistress' legs, who kicks and whips him. However, the players have struck these buffooneries (which indeed were calculated merely for the dregs of the people) out of Otway's tragedy; but they have still left in Shakspeare's Julius Caesar the jokes of the Roman shoemakers and cobblers, who are introduced in the same scene with Brutus and Cassius. You will undoubtedly complain, that those who have hitherto discoursed with you on the English stage, and especially on the celebrated Shakspeare, have taken notice only of his errors; and that on one has translated any of those strong, those forcible passages which atone for all his faults. But to this I will answer, that nothing is easier than to exhibit in prose all the silly impertinences which a poet may have thrown out; but that it is a very difficult task to translate his fine verses. All your junior academical sophs, who set up for censors of the eminent writers, compile whole volumes; but methinks two pages which display some of the beauties of great geniuses, are of infinitely more value than all the idle rhapsodies of those commentators; and I will join in opinion with all persons of good taste in declaring, that greater advantage may be reaped from a dozen verses of Homer or Virgil, than from all the critiques put together which have been made on those two great poets.

I have ventured to translate some passages of the most celebrated English poets, and shall now give you one from Shakspeare. Pardon the blemishes of the translation for the sake of the original; and remember always that when you see a version, you see merely a faint print of a beautiful picture. I have made choice of part of the celebrated soliloquy in Hamlet, which you may remember is as follows:

> "To be, or not to be? that is the question! Whether 't is nobler in the mind to suffer The slings and arrows of outrageous fortune, Or to take arms against a sea of troubles, And by opposing, end them? To die! to sleep! No more! and by a sleep to say we end The heart-ache, and the thousand natural shocks That flesh is heir to! 'T is a consummation Devoutly to be wished. To die! to sleep! To sleep; perchance to dream! Ay, there's the rub; For in that sleep of death, what dreams may come When we have shuffled off this mortal coil, Must give us pause. There 's the respect

Letters on the English; or Lettres Philosophiques

That makes a calamity of so long life: For who would bear the whips and scorns of time, The oppressor's wrong, the poor man's contumely, The pangs of despised love, the law's delay, The insolence of office, and the spurns That patient merit of the unworthy takes, When he himself might his quietus make With a bare bodkin. Who would fardels bear To groan and sweat under a weary life, But that the dread of something after death, The undiscovered country, from whose bourn No traveller returns, puzzles the will, And makes us rather bear those ills we have, Than fly to others that we know not of? Thus conscience does make cowards of us all; And thus the native hue of resolution Is sicklied o'er with the pale cast of thought: And enterprises of great weight and moment With this regard their currents turn awry, And lose the name of action–"

My version of it runs thus:

"Demeure, il faut choisir et passer a l'instant De la vie a la mort, ou de l'etre au neant. Dieux cruels, s'il en est, eclairez mon courage. Faut–il vieillir courbe sous la main qui m'outrage, Supporter, ou finir mon malheur et mon sort? Qui suis je? Qui m'arrete! et qu'est–ce que la mort? C'est la fin de nos maux, c'est mon unique asile Apres de longs transports, c'est un sommeil tranquile. On s'endort, et tout meurt, mais un affreux reveil Doit succeder peut etre aux douceurs du sommeil! On nous menace, on dit que cette courte vie, De tourmens eternels est aussi–tot suivie. O mort! moment fatal! affreuse eternite! Tout coeur a ton seul nom se glace epouvante. Eh! qui pourroit sans toi supporter cette vie, De nos pretres menteurs benir l'hypocrisie; D'une indigne maitresse encenser les erreurs, Ramper sous un ministre, adorer ses hauteurs; Et montrer les langueurs de son ame abattue, A des amis ingrats qui detournent la vue? La mort seroit trop douce en ces extremitez, Mais le scrupule parle, et nous crie, arretez; Il defend a nos mains cet heureux homicide Et d'un heros guerrier, fait un Chretien timide," &c.

Do not imagine that I have translated Shakspeare in a servile manner. Woe to the writer who gives a literal version; who by rendering every word of his original, by that very means enervates the sense, and extinguishes all the fire of it. It is on such an occasion one may justly affirm, that the letter kills, but the Spirit quickens.

Letters on the English; or Lettres Philosophiques

Here follows another passage copied from a celebrated tragic writer among the English. It is Dryden, a poet in the reign of Charles II.–a writer whose genius was too exuberant, and not accompanied with judgment enough. Had he written only a tenth part of the works he left behind him, his character would have been conspicuous in every part; but his great fault is his having endeavoured to be universal.

The passage in question is as follows:

> "When I consider life, 't is all a cheat, Yet fooled by hope, men favour the deceit; Trust on and think, to–morrow will repay; To–morrow's falser than the former day; Lies more; and whilst it says we shall be blest With some new joy, cuts off what we possessed; Strange cozenage! none would live past years again, Yet all hope pleasure in what yet remain, And from the dregs of life think to receive What the first sprightly running could not give. I'm tired with waiting for his chymic gold, Which fools us young, and beggars us when old."

I shall now give you my translation:

> "De desseins en regrets et d'erreurs en desirs Les mortels insenses promenent leur folie. Dans des malheurs presents, dans l'espoir des plaisirs Nous ne vivons jamais, nous attendons la vie. Demain, demain, dit–on, va combler tous nos voeus. Demain vient, et nous laisse encore plus malheureux. Quelle est l'erreur, helas! du soin qui nous devore, Nul de nous ne voudroit recommencer son cours. De nos premiers momens nous maudissons l'aurore, Et de la nuit qui vient nous attendons encore, Ce qu'ont en vain promis les plus beaux de nos jours," &c.

It is in these detached passages that the English have hitherto excelled. Their dramatic pieces, most of which are barbarous and without decorum, order, or verisimilitude, dart such resplendent flashes through this gleam, as amaze and astonish. The style is too much inflated, too unnatural, too closely copied from the Hebrew writers, who abound so much with the Asiatic fustian. But then it must be also confessed that the stilts of the figurative style, on which the English tongue is lifted up, raises the genius at the same time very far aloft, though with an irregular pace. The first English writer who composed a regular tragedy, and infused a spirit of elegance through every part of it, was the illustrious Mr.

Letters on the English; or Lettres Philosophiques

Addison. His "Cato" is a masterpiece, both with regard to the diction and to the beauty and harmony of the numbers. The character of Cato is, in my opinion, vastly superior to that of Cornelia in the "Pompey" of Corneille, for Cato is great without anything like fustian, and Cornelia, who besides is not a necessary character, tends sometimes to bombast. Mr. Addison's Cato appears to me the greatest character that was ever brought upon any stage, but then the rest of them do not correspond to the dignity of it, and this dramatic piece, so excellently well writ, is disfigured by a dull love plot, which spreads a certain languor over the whole, that quite murders it.

The custom of introducing love at random and at any rate in the drama passed from Paris to London about 1660, with our ribbons and our perruques. The ladies who adorn the theatrical circle there, in like manner as in this city will suffer love only to be the theme of every conversation. The judicious Mr. Addison had the effeminate complaisance to soften the severity of his dramatic character, so as to adapt it to the manners of the age, and, from an endeavour to please, quite ruined a masterpiece in its kind. Since is time the drama is become more regular, the audience more difficult to be leased, and writers more correct and less bold. I have seen some new pieces hat were written with great regularity, but which, at the same time, were ery flat and insipid. One would think that the English had been hitherto ormed to produce irregular beauties only. The shining monsters of Shakspeare ive infinite more delight than the judicious images of the moderns. Hitherto he poetical genius of the English resembles a tufted tree planted by the hand of Nature, that throws out a thousand branches at random, and spreads nequally, but with great vigour. It dies if you attempt to force its nature, and to lop and dress it in the same manner as the trees of the Garden of Marli.

Letter XIX: On Comedy

I am suprised that the judicious and ingenious Mr. de Muralt, who has published some letters on the English and French nations, should have confined himself, in treating of comedy, merely to censure Shadwell the comic writer. This author was had in pretty great contempt in Mr. de Muralt's time, and was not the poet of the polite part of the nation. His dramatic pieces, which pleased some time in acting, were despised by all persons of taste, and might be compared to many plays which I have seen France, that drew crowds

Letters on the English; or Lettres Philosophiques

to the play-house, at the same time that they were intolerable to read; and of which it might be said, that the whole city of Paris exploded them, and yet all flocked to see them represented on the stage. Methinks Mr. de Muralt should have mentioned an excellent comic writer (living when he was in England), I mean Mr. Wycherley, who was a long time known publicly to be happy in the good graces of the most celebrated mistress of King Charles II. This gentleman, who passed his life among persons of the highest distinction, was perfectly well acquainted with their lives and their follies, and painted them with the strongest pencil, and in the truest colours. He has drawn a misanthrope or man-hater, in imitation of that of Moliere. All Wycherley's strokes are stronger and bolder than those of our misanthrope, but then they are less delicate, and the rules of decorum are not so well observed in this play. The English writer has corrected the only defect that is in Moliere's comedy, the thinness of the plot, which also is so disposed that the characters in it do not enough raise our concern. The English comedy affects us, and the contrivance of the plot is very ingenious, but at the same time it is too bold for the French manners. The fable is this:—A captain of a man-of-war, who is very brave, open-hearted, and inflamed with a spirit of contempt for all mankind, has a prudent, sincere friend, whom he yet is suspicious of, and a mistress that loves him with the utmost excess of passion. The captain so far from returning her love, will not even condescend to look upon her, but confides entirely in a false friend, who is the most worthless wretch living. At the same time he has given his heart to a creature, who is the greatest coquette and the most perfidious of her sex, and he is so credulous as to be confident she is Penelope, and his false friend a Cato. He embarks on board his ship in order to go and fight the Dutch, having left all his money, his jewels, and everything he had in the world to this virtuous creature, whom at the same time he recommends to the care of his supposed faithful friend. Nevertheless the real man of honour, whom he suspects so unaccountably, goes on board the ship with him, and the mistress, on whom he would not bestow so much as one glance, disguises herself in the habit of a page, and is with him the whole voyage, without his once knowing that she is of a sex different from that she attempts to pass for, which, by the way, is not over natural.

The captain having blown up his own ship in an engagement, returns to England abandoned and undone, accompanied by his page and his friend, without knowing the friendship of the one or the tender passion of the other. Immediately he goes to the jewel among women, how he expected had preserved her fidelity to him and the treasure he had left in her hands. He meets with her indeed, but married to the honest knave in whom he had reposed so much confidence, and finds she had acted as treacherously with regard to the casket he had entrusted her with. The captain can scarce think it possible that a woman of virtue and honour can act so vile a part; but to convince him still more of the reality of it, this very worthy lady falls in love with the little page, and will force him to her embraces. But as it is requisite justice should be done, and that in a dramatic piece virtue ought to be rewarded and vice punished, it is at last found that the captain takes his page's place and lies with his faithless mistress, cuckolds his treacherous friend, thrusts his sword through his body, recovers his casket, and marries his page. You will observe that this play is also larded with a petulant, litigious old woman (a relation of the captain), who is the most comical character that was ever brought upon the stage.

Wycherley has also copied from Moliere another play, of as singular and bold a cast, which is a kind of Ecole des Femmes, or, School for Married Women.

The principal character in this comedy isone Horner, a sly fortune hunter, and the terror of all the City husbands. This fellow, in order to play a surer game, causes a report to be spread, that in his last illness, the surgeons had found it necessary to have him made a eunuch. Upon his appearing in this noble character, all the husbands in town flocked to him with their wives, and now poor Horner is only puzzled about his choice. However, he gives the preference particularly to a little female peasant, a very harmless, innocent creature, who enjoys a fine flush of health, and cuckolds her husband with a simplicity that has infinitely more merit than the witty malice of the most experienced ladies. This play cannot indeed be called the school of good morals, but it is certainly the school of wit and true humour.

Sir John Vanbrugh has written several comedies, which are more humorous than those of Mr. Wycherley, but not so ingenious. Sir John was a man of pleasure, and likewise a poet and an architect. The general opinion is, that he is as sprightly in his writings as he is heavy in his buildings. It is he who raised the famous Castle of Blenheim, a ponderous and lasting monument of our unfortunate Battle of Hochstet. Were the apartments but as spacious as the walls are thick, this castle would be commodious enough. Some wag, in an epitaph he made on Sir John Vanbrugh, has these lines:

"Earth lie light on him, for he Laid many a heavy load in thee."

Sir John having taken a tour into France before the glorious war that broke out in 1701, was thrown into the Bastille, and detained there for some time, without being ever able to discover the motive which had prompted our ministry to indulge him with this mark of their distinction. He wrote a comedy during his confinement; and a circumstance which appears to me very extraordinary is, that we don't meet with so much as a single satirical stroke against the country in which he had been so injuriously treated.

The late Mr. Congreve raised the glory of comedy to a greater height than any English writer before or since his time. He wrote only a few plays, but they are all excellent in their kind. The laws of the drama are strictly observed in them; they abound with characters all which are shadowed with the utmost delicacy, and we don't meet with so much as one low or coarse jest. The language is everywhere that of men of honour, but their actions are those of knaves—a proof that he was perfectly well acquainted with human nature, and frequented what we call polite company. He was infirm and come to the verge of life when I knew him. Mr. Congreve had one defect, which was his entertaining too mean an idea of his first profession (that of a writer), though it was to this he owed his fame and fortune. He spoke of his works as of trifles that were beneath him; and hinted to me, in our first conversation, that I should visit him upon no other footing than that of a gentleman who led a life of plainness and simplicity. I answered, that had he been so unfortunate as to be a mere gentleman, I should never have come to see him; and I was very much disgusted at so unseasonable a piece of vanity.

Mr. Congreve's comedies are the most witty and regular, those of Sir John Vanbrugh most gay and humorous, and those of Mr. Wycherley have the greatest force and spirit. It may be proper to observe that these fine geniuses never spoke disadvantageously of Moliere; and that none but the contemptible writers among the English have endeavoured to lessen the character of that great comic poet. Such Italian musicians as despise Lully are themselves persons of no character or ability; but a Buononcini esteems that great artist, and does justice to his merit.

The English have some other good comic writers living, such as Sir Richard Steele and Mr. Cibber, who is an excellent player, and also Poet Laureate—a title which, how ridiculous soever it may be thought, is yet worth a thousand crowns a year (besides some considerable privileges) to the person who enjoys it. Our illustrious Corneille had not so much.

To conclude. Don't desire me to descend to particulars with regard to these English comedies, which I am so fond of applauding; nor to give you a single smart saying or humorous stroke from Wycherley or Congreve. We don't laugh in reading a translation. If you have a mind to understand the English comedy, the only way to do this will be for you to go to England, to spend three years in London, to make yourself master of the English tongue, and to frequent the playhouse every night. I receive but little pleasure from the perusal of Aristophanes and Plautus, and for this reason because I am neither a Greek nor a Roman. The delicacy of the humour, the allusion, the a propos—all these are lost to a foreigner.

But it is different with respect to tragedy, this treating only of exalted passions and heroical follies, which the antiquated errors of fable or history have made sacred. Oedipus, Electra, and such-like characters, may with as much propriety be treated of by the Spaniards, the English, or us, as by the Greeks. But true comedy is the speaking picture of the follies and ridiculous foibles of a nation; so that he only is able to judge of the painting who is perfectly acquainted with the people it represents.

Letter XX: On Such Of The Nobility As Cultivate The Belles Lettres

There once was a time in France when the polite arts were cultivated by persons of the highest rank in the state. The courtiers particularly were conversant in them, although indolence, a taste for trifles, and a passion for intrigue, were the divinities of the country. The Court methinks at this time seems to have given into a taste quite opposite to that of polite literature, but perhaps the mode of thinking may be revived in a little time. The French are of so flexible a disposition, may be moulded into such a variety of shapes, that the monarch needs but command and he is immediately obeyed. The English generally think, and learning is had in greater honour among them than in our country – an advantage that results naturally from the form of their government. There are about eight hundred persons in England who have a right to speak in public, and to support the interest of the kingdom and near five or six thousand may in their turns aspire to the same honour. The whole nation set themselves up as judges over these, and every man has the liberty of publishing his thoughts with regard to public affairs, which shows that all the people in general are indispensably obliged to cultivate their understandings. In England the governments of Greece and Rome are the subject of every conversation, so that every

Letters on the English; or Lettres Philosophiques

man is under a necessity of perusing such authors as treat of them, how disagreeable soever it may be to him; and this study leads naturally to that of polite literature. Mankind in general speak well in their respective professions. What is the reason why our magistrates, our lawyers, our physicians, and a great number of the clergy, are abler scholars, have a finer taste, and more wit, than persons of all other professions? The reason is, because their condition of life requires a cultivated and enlightened mind, in the same manner as a merchant is obliged to be acquainted with his traffic. Not long since an English nobleman, who was very young, came to see me at Paris on his return from Italy. He had written a poetical description of that country, which, for delicacy and politeness, may vie with anything we meet with in the Earl of Rochester, or in our Chaulieu, our Sarrasin, or Chapelle. The translation I have given of it is so inexpressive of the strength and delicate humour of the original, that I am obliged seriously to ask pardon of the author and of all who understand English. However, as this is the only method I have to make his lordship's verses known, I shall here present you with them in our tongue:

> "Qu'ay je donc vu dans l'Italie? Orgueil, astuce, et pauvrete, Grands complimens, peu de bonte Et beaucoup de ceremonie

> "L'extravagante comedie Que souvent l'Inquisition Veut qu'on nomme religion Mais qu'ici nous nommons folie.

> "La Nature en vain bienfaisante Veut enricher ses lieux charmans, Des pretres la main desolante Etouffe ses plus beaux presens.

> "Les monsignors, soy disant Grands, Seuls dans leurs palais magnifiques Y sont d'illustres faineants, Sans argent, et sans domestiques.

> "Pour les petits, sans liberte, Martyrs du joug qui les domine, Ils ont fait voeu de pauvrete, Priant Dieu par oisivete Et toujours jeunant par famine.

> "Ces beaux lieux du Pape benis Semblent habitez par les diables; Et les habitans miserables Sont damnes dans le Paradis."

Letters on the English; or Lettres Philosophiques

Letter XXI: On The Earl Of Rochester And Mr. Waller

The Earl of Rochester's name is universally known. Mr. de St. Evremont has made very frequent mention of him, but then he has represented this famous nobleman in no other light than as the man of pleasure, as one who was the idol of the fair; but, with regard to myself, I would willingly describe in him the man of genius, the great poet. Among other pieces which display the shining imagination his lordship only could boast, he wrote some satires on the same subjects as those our celebrated Boileau made choice of. I do not know any better method of improving the taste than to compare the productions of such great geniuses as have exercised their talent on the same subject. Boileau declaims as follows against human reason in his "Satire on Man":

> "Cependant a le voir plein de vapeurs legeres, Soi–meme se bercer de ses propres chimeres, Lui seul de la nature est la baze et l'appui, Et le dixieme ciel ne tourne que pour lui. De tous les animaux il est ici le maitre; Qui pourroit le nier, poursuis tu? Moi peut–etre Ce maitre pretendu qui leur donne des loix, Ce roi des animaux, combien a–t'il de rois?"

> "Yet, pleased with idle whimsies of his brain, And puffed with pride, this haughty thing would fain Be think himself the only stay and prop That holds the mighty frame of Nature up. The skies and stars his properties must seem,

* * * * * * * *

Of all the creatures he's the lord, he cries.

* * * * * * * *

And who is there, say you, that dares deny So owned a truth? That may be, sir, do I.

* * * * * * * *

This boasted monarch of the world who awes The creatures here, and with his nod gives

Letters on the English; or Lettres Philosophiques

laws This self-named king, who thus pretends to be The lord of all, how many lords has he?"

Oldham, a little altered.

The Lord Rochester expresses himself, in his "Satire against Man," in pretty near the following manner. But I must first desire you always to remember that the versions I give you from the English poets are written with freedom and latitude, and that the restraint of our versification, and the delicacies of the French tongue, will not allow a translator to convey into it the licentious impetuosity and fire of the English numbers:

"Cet esprit que je hais, cet esprit plein d'erreur, Ce n'est pas ma raison c'est la tienne, docteur C'est la raison frivole, inquiete, orgueilleuse Des sages animaux, rivale dedaigneuse, Qui croit entr'eux et l'Ange, occuper le milieu, Et pense etre ici bas l'image de son Dieu. Vil atome imparfait, qui croit, doute, dispute Rampe, s'eleve, tombe, et nie encore sa chute, Qui nous dit je suis libre, en nous montrant ses fers, Et dont l'oeil, trouble et faux, croit percer l'univers. Allez, reverends fous, bienheureux fanatiques, Compilez bien l'amas de vos riens scholastiques, Peres de visions, et d'enigmes sacres, Auteurs du labirinthe, ou vous vous egarez. Allez obscurement eclaircir vos misteres, Et courez dans l'ecole adorer vos chimeres. Il est d'autres erreurs, il est de ces devots Condamne par eux memes a l'ennui du repos. Ce mystique encloitre, fier de son indolence Tranquille, au sein de Dieu. Que peut il faire? Il pense. Non, tu ne penses point, miserable, tu dors: Inutile a la terre, et mis au rang des morts. Ton esprit enerve croupit dans la molesse. Reveille toi, sois homme, et sors de ton ivresse. L'homme est ne pour agir, et tu pretens penser?" &c.

The original runs thus:

"Hold mighty man, I cry all this we know, And 'tis this very reason I despise, This supernatural gift that makes a mite Think he's the image of the Infinite; Comparing his short life, void of all rest, To the eternal and the ever blest. This busy, puzzling stirrer up of doubt, That frames deep mysteries, then finds them out, Filling, with frantic crowds of thinking fools, Those reverend bedlams, colleges, and schools; Borne on whose wings each heavy sot can pierce The limits of the boundless universe. So charming ointments make an old witch fly, And bear a crippled carcass through the sky. 'Tis this exalted power, whose business lies In nonsense and impossibilities. This made a whimsical philosopher Before the spacious world his tub prefer; And we have modern cloistered coxcombs, who Retire to think, 'cause they have naught to do. But thoughts are given for action's government, Where action ceases, thought's impertinent."

Whether these ideas are true or false, it is certain they are expressed with an energy and fire which form the poet. I shall be very far from attempting to examine philosophically into these verses, to lay down the pencil, and take up the rule and compass on this occasion; my only design in this letter being to display the genius of the English poets, and therefore I shall continue in the same view.

The celebrated Mr. Waller has been very much talked of in France, and Mr. de la Fontaine, St. Evremont, and Bayle have written his eulogium, but still his name only is known. He had much the same reputation in London as Voiture had in Paris, and in my opinion deserved it better. Voiture was born in an age that was just emerging from barbarity; an age that was still rude and ignorant, the people of which aimed at wit, though they had not the least pretensions to it, and sought for points and conceits instead of sentiments. Bristol stones are more easily found than diamonds. Voiture, born with an easy and frivolous genius, was the first who shone in this aurora of French literature. Had he come into the world after those great geniuses who spread such a glory over the age of Louis XIV., he would either have been unknown, would have been despised, or would have corrected his style. Boileau applauded him, but it was in his first satires, at a time when the taste of that great poet was not yet formed. He was young, and in an age when persons form a judgment of men from their reputation, and not from their writings. Besides, Boileau was very partial both in his encomiums and his censures. He applauded Segrais, whose works nobody reads; he abused Quinault, whose poetical pieces every one has got by heart; and is wholly silent upon La Fontaine. Waller, though a better poet than Voiture, was not yet a finished poet. The graces breathe in such of Waller's works as are writ in a tender strain; but then they are languid through negligence, and often disfigured with false thoughts. The English had not in his time attained the art of correct writing. But his serious compositions exhibit a strength and vigour which could not have been

Letters on the English; or Lettres Philosophiques

expected from the softness and effeminacy of his other pieces. He wrote an elegy on Oliver Cromwell, which, with all its faults, is nevertheless looked upon as a masterpiece. To understand this copy of verses you are to know that the day Oliver died was remarkable for a great storm. His poem begins in this manner:

"Il n'est plus, s'en est fait, soumettons nous au sort, Le ciel a signale ce jour par des tempetes, Et la voix des tonnerres eclatant sur nos tetes Vient d'annoncer sa mort.

"Par ses derniers soupirs il ebranle cet ile; Cet ile que son bras fit trembler tant de fois, Quand dans le cours de ses exploits, Il brisoit la tete des Rois, Et soumettoit un peuple a son joug seul docile.

"Mer tu t'en es trouble; O mer tes flots emus Semblent dire en grondant aux plus lointains rivages Que l'effroi de la terre et ton maitre n'est plus.

"Tel au ciel autrefois s'envola Romulus, Tel il quitta la Terre, au milieu des orages, Tel d'un peuple guerrier il recut les homages; Obei dans sa vie, a sa mort adore, Son palais fut un Temple," &c.

"We must resign! heaven his great soul does claim In storms as loud as his immortal fame; His dying groans, his last breath shakes our isle, And trees uncut fall for his funeral pile: About his palace their broad roots are tost Into the air; so Romulus was lost! New Rome in such a tempest missed her king, And from obeying fell to worshipping. On Oeta's top thus Hercules lay dead, With ruined oaks and pines about him spread. Nature herself took notice on his death, And, sighing, swelled the sea with such a breath, That to remotest shores the billows rolled, Th' approaching fate of his great ruler told."

Waller.

It was this eulogium that gave occasion to the reply (taken notice of in Bayle's Dictionary), which Waller made to King Charles II. This king, to whom Waller had a little before (as is usual with bards and monarchs) presented a copy of verses embroidered with praises, reproached the poet for not writing with so much energy and fire as when he had applauded the Usurper (meaning Oliver). "Sir," replied Waller to the king, "we poets succeed better in fiction than in truth." This answer was not so sincere as that which a Dutch Ambassador made, who, when the same monarch complained that his masters paid less regard to him than they had done to Cromwell: "Ah, sir!" says the Ambassador, "Oliver was quite another man___." It is not my intent to give a commentary on Waller's character, nor on that of any other person; for I consider men after their death in no other light than as they were writers, and wholly disregard everything else. I shall only observe that Waller, though born in a Court, and to an estate of five or six thousand pounds sterling a year, was never so proud or so indolent as to lay aside the happy talent which Nature had indulged him. The Earls of Dorset and Roscommon, the two Dukes of Buckingham, the Lord Halifax, and so many other noblemen, did not think the reputation they obtained of very great poets and illustrious writers, any way derogatory to their quality. They are more glorious for their works than for their titles. These cultivated the polite arts with as much assiduity as though they had been their whole dependence. They also have made learning appear venerable in the eyes of the vulgar, who have need to be led in all things by the great; and who, nevertheless, fashion their manners less after those of the nobility (in England I mean) than in any other country in the world.

Letter XXII: On Mr. Pope And Some Other Famous Poets

In intended to treat of Mr. Prior, one of the most amiable English poets, whom you saw Plenipotentiary and Envoy Extraordinary at Paris in 1712. I also designed to have given you some idea of the Lord Roscommon's and the Lord Dorset's muse; but I find that to do this I should be obliged to write a large volume, and that, after much pains and trouble, you would have but an imperfect idea of all those works. Poetry is a kind of music in which a man should have some knowledge before he pretends to judge of it. When I give you a translation of some passages from those foreign poets, I only prick down, and that imperfectly, their music; but then I cannot express the taste of their harmony.

There is one English poem especially which I should despair of ever making you understand, the title whereof is "Hudibras." The subject of it is the Civil War in the time of the grand rebellion, and the principles and practice of the Puritans are therein ridiculed.

Letters on the English; or Lettres Philosophiques

It is Don Quixote, it is our "Satire Menippee" blended together. I never found so much wit in one single book as in that, which at the same time is the most difficult to be translated. Who would believe that a work which paints in such lively and natural colours the several foibles and follies of mankind, and where we meet with more sentiments than words, should baffle the endeavours of the ablest translator? But the reason of this is, almost every part of it alludes to particular incidents. The clergy are there made the principal object of ridicule, which is understood but by few among the laity. To explain this a commentary would be requisite, and humour when explained is no longer humour. Whoever sets up for a commentator of smart sayings and repartees is himself a blockhead. This is the reason why the works of the ingenious Dean Swift, who has been called the English Rabelais, will never be well understood in France. This gentleman has the honour (in common with Rabelais) of being a priest, and, like him, laughs at everything; but, in my humble opinion, the title of the English aebelais which is given the dean is highly derogatory to his genius. The former has interspersed his unaccountably fantastic and unitelligible book with the most gay strokes of humour; but which at the same time, has a greater proportion of impertinence. He has been vastly lavish of erudition, of smut, and insipid raillery. An agreeable tale of two pages is purchased at the expense of whole volumes of nonsense. There are but few persons, and those of a grotesque taste, who pretend to understand and to esteem this work; for, as to the rest of the nation, they laugh at the pleasant and diverting touches which are found in Rabelais and despise his book. He is looked upon as the prince of buffoons. The readers are vexed to think that a man who was master of so much wit should have made so wretched a use of it; he is an intoxicated philosopher who never wrote but when he was in liquor.

Dean Swift is Rabelais in his senses, and frequently the politest company. The former, indeed, is not so gay as the latter, but then he possesses all the delicacy, the justness, the choice, the good taste, in all which particulars our giggling rural Vicar Rabelais is wanting. The poetical numbers of Dean Swift are of a singular and almost inimitable taste; true humour, whether in prose or verse, seems to be his peculiar talent; but whoever is desirous of understanding him perfectly must visit the island in which he was born.

It will be much easier for you to form an idea of Mr. Pope's works. He is, in my opinion, the most elegant, the most correct poet; and, at the same time, the most harmonious (a circumstance which redounds very much to the honour of this muse) that England ever gave birth to. He has mellowed the harsh sounds of the English trumpet to the soft accents of the flute. His compositions may be easily translated, because they are vastly

Letters on the English; or Lettres Philosophiques

clear and perspicuous; besides, most of his subjects are general, and relative to all nations.

His "Essay on Criticism" will soon be known in France by the translation which l'Abbe de Renel has made of it.

Here is an extract from his poem entitled the "Rape of the Lock," which I just now translated with the latitude I usually take on these occasions; for, once again, nothing can be more ridiculous than to translate a poet literally:

> "Umbriel, a l'instant, vieil gnome rechigne, Va d'une aile pesante et d'un air renfrogne Chercher en murmurant la caverne profonde, Ou loin des doux raions que repand l'oeil du monde La Deesse aux Vapeurs a choisi son sejour, Les Tristes Aquilons y sifflent a l'entour, Et le souffle mal sain de leur aride haleine Y porte aux environs la fievre et la migraine. Sur un riche sofa derriere un paravent Loin des flambeaux, du bruit, des parleurs et du vent La quinteuse deesse incessamment repose, Le coeur gros de chagrin, sans en savoir la cause. N'aiant pense jamais, l'esprit toujours trouble, L'oceil charge, le teint pale, et l'hypocondre enfle. La medisante Envie, est assise aupres d'elle, Vieil spectre feminin, decrepite pucelle, Avec un air devot dechirant son prochain, Et chansonnant les Gens l'Evangile a la main. Sur un lit plein de fleurs negligemment panchee Une jeune beaute non loin d'elle est couchee, C'est l'Afectation qui grassaie en parlant, Ecoute sans entendre, et lorgne en regardant. Qui rougit sans pudeur, et rit de tout sans joie, De cent maux differens pretend qu'elle est la proie; Et pleine de sante sous le rouge et le fard, Se plaint avec molesse, et se pame avec art."

> "Umbriel, a dusky, melancholy sprite As ever sullied the fair face of light, Down to the central earth, his proper scene, Repairs to search the gloomy cave of Spleen, Swift on his sooty pinions flits the gnome, And in a vapour reached the dismal dome, No cheerful breeze this sullen region knows, The dreaded east is all the wind that blows. Here, in a grotto, sheltered close from air, And screened in shades from day's detested glare, She sighs for ever on her pensive bed, Pain at her side, and Megrim at her head, Two handmaids wait the throne. Alike in place,

Letters on the English; or Lettres Philosophiques

But differing far in figure and in face, Here stood Ill-nature, like an ancient maid, Her wrinkled form in black and white arrayed; With store of prayers for mornings, nights, and noons Her hand is filled; her bosom with lampoons. There Affectation, with a sickly mien, Shows in her cheek the roses of eighteen, Practised to lisp, and hang the head aside, Faints into airs, and languishes with pride; On the rich quilt sinks with becoming woe, Wrapt in a gown, for sickness and for show."

This extract, in the original (not in the faint translation I have given you of it), may be compared to the description of La Molesse (softness or effeminacy), in Boileau's "Lutrin."

Methinks I now have given you specimens enough from the English poets. I have made some transient mention of their philosophers, but as for good historians among them, I don't know of any; and, indeed, a Frenchman was forced to write their history. Possibly the English genius, which is either languid or impetuous, has not yet acquired that unaffected eloquence, that plain but majestic air which history requires. Possibly too, the spirit of party which exhibits objects in a dim and confused light may have sunk the credit of their historians. One half of the nation is always at variance with the other half. I have met with people who assured me that the Duke of Marlborough was a coward, and that Mr. Pope was a fool; just as some Jesuits in France declare Pascal to have been a man of little or no genius, and some Jansenists affirm Father Bourdaloue to have been a mere babbler. The Jacobites consider Mary Queen of Scots as a pious heroine, but those of an opposite party look upon her as a prostitute, an adulteress, a murderer. Thus the English have memorials of the several reigns, but no such thing as a history. There is, indeed, now living, one Mr. Gordon (the public are obliged to him for a translation of Tacitus), who is very capable of writing the history of his own country, but Rapin de Thoyras got the start of him. To conclude, in my opinion the English have not such good historians as the French, have no such thing as a real tragedy, have several delightful comedies, some wonderful passages in certain of their poems, and boast of philosophers that are worthy writers of our nation, and therefore we ought (since they have not scrupled to be in our debt) to borrow from them. Both the English and we came after the Italians, who have been our instructors in all the arts, and whom we have surpassed in some. I cannot determine which of the three nations ought to be honoured with the palm; but happy the writer who could display their various merits.

Letters on the English; or Lettres Philosophiques

Letter XXIII: On The Regard That Ought To Be Shown To Men Of Letters

Neither the English nor any other people have foundations established in favour of the polite arts like those in France. There are Universities in most countries, but it is in France only that we meet with so beneficial an encouragement for astronomy and all parts of the mathematics, for physic, for researches into antiquity, for painting, sculpture, and architecture. Louis XIV. has immortalised his name by these several foundations, and this immortality did not cost him two hundred thousand livres a year.

I must confess that one of the things I very much wonder at is, that as the Parliament of Great Britain have promised a reward of 20,000 pounds sterling to any person who may discover the longitude, they should never have once thought to imitate Louis XIV. in his munificence with regard to the arts and sciences.

Merit, indeed, meets in England with rewards of another kind, which redound more to the honour of the nation. The English have so great a veneration for exalted talents, that a man of merit in their country is always sure of making his fortune. Mr. Addison in France would have been elected a member of one of the academies, and, by the credit of some women, might have obtained a yearly pension of twelve hundred livres, or else might have been imprisoned in the Bastile, upon pretence that certain strokes in his tragedy of Cato had been discovered which glanced at the porter of some man in power. Mr. Addison was raised to the post of Secretary of State in England. Sir Isaac Newton was made Warden of the Royal Mint. Mr. Congrefe has a considerable employment. Mr. Prior was Plenipotentiary. Dr. Swift is Dean of St. Patrick in Dublin, and is more revered in Ireland than the Primate himself. The religion which Mr. Pope professes excludes him, indeed from preferments of every kind, but then it did not prevent his gaining two hundred thousand livres by his excellent translation of Homer. I myself saw a long time in France the author of Rhadamistus ready to perish for hunger. And the son of one of the greatest men our country ever gave birth to, and who was beginning to run the noble career which his father had set him, would have been reduced to the extremes of misery had he not been patronised by Monsieur Fagon.

Letters on the English; or Lettres Philosophiques

But the circumstance which mostly encourages the arts in England is the great veneration which is paid them. The picture of the Prime Minister hangs over the chimney of his own closet, but I have seen that of Mr. Pope in twenty noblemen's houses. Sir Isaac Newton was revered in his lifetime, and had a due respect paid to him after his death; the greatest men in the nation disputing who should have the honour of holding up his pall. Go into Westminster Abbey, and you will find that what raises the admiration of the spectator is not the mausoleums of the English kings, but the monuments which the gratitude of the nation has erected to perpetuate the memory of those illustrious men who contributed to its glory. We view their statues in that abbey in the same manner as those of Sophocles, Plato, and other immortal personages were viewed in Athens; and I am persuaded that the bare sight of those glorious monuments has fired more than one breast, and been the occasion of their becoming great men.

The English have even been reproached with paying too extravagant honours to mere merit, and censured for interring the celebrated actress Mrs. Oldfield in Westminster Abbey with almost the same pomp as Sir Isaac Newton. Some pretend that the English had paid her these great funeral honours, purposely to make us more strongly sensible of the barbarity and injustice which they object to in us, for having buried Mademoiselle Le Couvreur ignominiously in the fields.

But be assured from me, that the English were prompted by no other principle in burying Mrs. Oldfield in Westminster Abbey than their good sense. They are far from being so ridiculous as to brand with infamy an art which has immortalised a Euripides and a Sophocles; or to exclude from the body of their citizens a set of people whose business is to set off with the utmost grace of speech and action those pieces which the nation is proud of.

Under the reign of Charles I. and in the beginning of the civil wars raised by a number of rigid fanatics, who at last were the victims to it; a great many pieces were published against theatrical and other shows, which were attacked with the greater virulence because that monarch and his queen, daughter to Henry IV. of France, were passionately fond of them.

One Mr. Prynne, a man of most furiously scrupulous principles, who would have thought himself damned had he worn a cassock instead of a short cloak, and have been glad to see one-half of mankind cut the other to pieces for the glory of God, and the Propaganda

Letters on the English; or Lettres Philosophiques

Fide; took it into his head to write a most wretched satire against some pretty good comedies, which were exhibited very innocently every night before their majesties. He quoted the authority of the Rabbis, and some passages from St. Bonaventure, to prove that the Cedipus of Sophocles was the work of the evil spirit; that Terence was excommunicated ipso facto; and added, that doubtless Brutus, who was a very severe Jansenist, assassinated Julius Caesar for no other reason but because he, who was Pontifex Maximus, presumed to write a tragedy the subject of which was Cedipus. Lastly, he declared that all who frequented the theatre were excommunicated, as they thereby renounced their baptism. This was casting the highest insult on the king and all the royal family; and as the English loved their prince at that time, they could not bear to hear a writer talk of excommunicating him, though they themselves afterwards cut his head off. Prynne was summoned to appear before the Star Chamber; his wonderful book, from which Father Le Brun stole his, was sentenced to be burnt by the common hangman, and himself to lose his ears. His trial is now extant.

The Italians are far from attempting to cast a blemish on the opera, or to excommunicate Signor Senesino or Signora Cuzzoni. With regard to myself, I could presume top wish that the magistrates would suppress I know not what contemptible pieces written against the stage. For when the English and Italians hear that we brand with the greatest mark of infamy an art in which we excel; that we excommunicate persons who receive salaries from the king; that we condemn as impious a spectacle exhibited in convents and monasteries; that we dishonour sports in which Louis XIV. and Louis XV. performed as actors; that we give the title of the devil's works to pieces which are received by magistrates of the most severe character, and represented before a virtuous queen; when, I say, foreigners are told of this insolent conduct, this contempt for the royal authority, and this Gothic rusticity which some presume to call Christian severity, what an idea must they entertain of our nation? And how will it be possible for them to conceive, either that our laws give a sanction to an art which is declared infamous, or that some persons dare to stamp with infamy an art which receives a sanction from the laws, is rewarded by kings, cultivated and encouraged by the greatest men, and admired by whole nations? And that Father Le Brun's impertinent libel against the stage is seen in a bookseller's shop' standing the very next to the immortal labours of Racine, of Corneille, of Moliere, &c.

Letters on the English; or Lettres Philosophiques

Letter XXIV: On The Royal Society And Other Academies

The English had an Academy of Sciences many years before us, but then it is not under such prudent regulations as ours, the only reason of which very possibly is, because it was founded before the Academy of Paris; for had it been founded after, it would very probably have adopted some of the sage laws of the former and improved upon others.

Two things, and those the most essential to man, are wanting in the Royal Society of London, I mean rewards and laws. A seat in the Academy at Paris is a small but secure fortune to a geometrician or a chemist; but this is so far from being the case at London, that the several members of the Royal Society are at a continual, though indeed small expense. Any man in England who declares himself a lover of the mathematics and natural philosophy, and expresses an inclination to be a member of the Royal Society, is immediately elected into it. But in France it is not enough that a man who aspires to the honour of being a member of the Academy, and of receiving the royal stipend, has a love for the sciences; he must at the same time be deeply skilled in them; and is obliged to dispute the seat with competitors who are so much the more formidable as they are fired by a principle of glory, by interest, by the difficulty itself, and by that inflexibility of mind which is generally found in those who devote themselves to that pertinacious study, the mathematics.

The Academy of Sciences is prudently confined to the study of Nature, and, indeed, this is a field spacious enough for fifty or three-score persons to range in. That of London mixes indiscriminately literature with physics; but methinks the founding an academy merely for the polite arts is more judicious, as it prevents confusion, and the joining, in some measure, of heterogeneals, such as a dissertation on the head-dresses of the Roman ladies with a hundred or more new curves.

As there is very little order and regularity in the Royal Society, and not the least encouragement; and that the Academy of Paris is on a quite different foot, it is no wonder that our transactions are drawn up in a more just and beautiful manner than those of the English. Soldiers who are under a regular discipline, and besides well paid, must necessarily at last perform more glorious achievements than others who are mere volunteers. It must indeed be confessed that the Royal Society boast their Newton, but then he did not owe his knowledge and discoveries to that body; so far from it, that the

Letters on the English; or Lettres Philosophiques

latter were intelligible to very few of his fellow members. A genius like that of Sir Isaac belonged to all the academies in the world, because all had a thousand things to learn of him.

The celebrated Dean Swift formed a design, in the latter end of the late Queen's reign, to found an academy for the English tongue upon the model of that of the French. This project was promoted by the late Earl of Oxford, Lord High Treasurer, and much more by the Lord Bolingbroke, Secretary of State, who had the happy talent of speaking without premeditation in the Parliament House with as much purity as Dean Swift wrote in his closet, and who would have been the ornament and protector of that academy. Those only would have been chosen members of it whose works will last as long as the English tongue, such as Dean Swift, Mr. Prior, whom we saw here invested with a public character, and whose fame in England is equal to that of La Fontaine in France; Mr. Pope, the English Boileau, Mr. Congreve, who may be called their Moliere, and several other eminent persons whose names I have forgot; all these would have raised the glory of that body to a great height even in its infancy. But Queen Anne being snatched suddenly from the world, the Whigs were resolved to ruin the protectors of the intended academy, a circumstance that was of the most fatal consequence to polite literature. The members of this academy would have had a very great advantage over those who first formed that of the French, for Swift, Prior, Congreve, Dryden, Pope, Addison, &c. had fixed the English tongue by their writings; whereas Chapelain, Colletet, Cassaigne, Faret, Perrin, Cotin, our first academicians, were a disgrace to their country; and so much ridicule is now attached to their very names, that if an author of some genius in this age had the misfortune to be called Chapelain or Cotin, he would be under a necessity of changing his name.

One circumstance, to which the English Academy should especially have attended, is to have prescribed to themselves occupations of a quite different kind from those with which our academicians amuse themselves. A wit of this country asked me for the memoirs of the French Academy. I answered, they have no memoirs, but have printed threescore or fourscore volumes in quarto of compliments. The gentleman perused one or two of them, but without being able to understand the style in which they were written; though he understood all our good authors perfectly. "All," says he, "I see in these elegant discourses is, that the member elect having assured the audience that his predecessor was a great man, that Cardinal Richelieu was a very great man, that the Chancellor Seguier was a pretty great man, that Louis XIV. was a more than great man, the director answers

Letters on the English; or Lettres Philosophiques

in the very same strain, and adds, that the member elect may also be a sort of great man, and that himself, in quality of director, must also have some share in this greatness."

The cause why all these academical discourses have unhappily done so little honour to this body is evident enough. Vitium est temporis potius quam hominis (the fault is owing to the age rather than to particular persons). It grew up insensibly into a custom for every academician to repeat these eulogiums at his reception; it was laid down as a kind of law that the public should be indulged from time to time in the sullen satisfaction of yawning over these productions. If the reason should afterwards be sought, why the greatest geniuses who have been incorporated into that body have sometimes made the worst speeches, I answer, that it is wholly owing to a strong propension, the gentlemen in question had to shine, and to display a thread-bare, worn-out subject in a new and uncommon light. The necessity of saying something, the perplexity of having nothing to say, and a desire of being witty, are three circumstances which alone are capable of making even the greatest writer ridiculous. These gentlemen, not being able to strike out any new thoughts, hunted after a new play of words, and delivered themselves without thinking at all: in like manner as people who should seem to chew with great eagerness, and make as though they were eating, at the same time that they were just starved.

It is a law in the French Academy, to publish all those discourses by which only they are known, but they should rather make a law never to print any of them.

But the Academy of the Belles Lettres have a more prudent and more useful object, which is, to present the public with a collection of transactions that abound with curious researches and critiques. These transactions are already esteemed by foreigners; and it were only to be wished that some subjects in them had been more thoroughly examined, and that others had not been treated at all. As, for instance, we should have been very well satisfied, had they omitted I know not what dissertation on the prerogative of the right hand over the left; and some others, which, though not published under so ridiculous a title, are yet written on subjects that are almost as frivolous and silly.

The Academy of Sciences, in such of their researches as are of a more difficult kind and a more sensible use, embrace the knowledge of nature and the improvements of the arts. We may presume that such profound, such uninterrupted pursuits as these, such exact calculations, such refined discoveries, such extensive and exalted views, will, at last, produce something that may prove of advantage to the universe. Hitherto, as we have observed together, the most useful discoveries have been made in the most barbarous times. One would conclude that the business of the most enlightened ages and the most learned bodies, is, to argue and debate on things which were invented by ignorant people. We know exactly the angle which the sail of a ship is to make with the keel in order to make its sailing better; and yet Columbus discovered America without having the least idea of the property of this angle: however, I am far from inferring from hence that we are to confine ourselves merely to a blind practice, but happy it were, would naturalists and geometricians unite, as much as possible, the practice with the theory.

Strange, but so it is, that those things which reflect the greatest honour on the human mind are frequently of the least benefit to it! A man who understands the four fundamental rules of arithmetic, aided by a little good sense, shall amass prodigious wealth in trade, shall become a Sir Peter Delme, a Sir Richard Hopkins, a Sir Gilbert Heathcote, whilst a poor algebraist spends his whole life in searching for astonishing properties and relations in numbers, which at the same time are of no manner of use, and will not acquaint him with the nature of exchanges. This is very nearly the case with most of the arts: there is a certain point beyond which all researches serve to no other purpose than merely to delight an inquisitive mind. Those ingenious and useless truths may be compared to stars which, by being placed at too great a distance, cannot afford us the least light.

With regard to the French Academy, how great a service would they do to literature, to the language, and the nation, if, instead of publishing a set of compliments annually, they would give us new editions of the valuable works written in the age of Louis XIV., purged from the several errors of diction which are crept into them. There are many of these errors in Corneille and Moliere, but those in La Fontaine are very numerous. Such as could not be corrected might at least be pointed out. By this means, as all the Europeans read those works, they would teach them our language in its utmost purity—which, by that means, would be fixed to a lasting standard; and valuable French books being then printed at the King's expense, would prove one of the most glorious monuments the nation could boast. I have been told that Boileau formerly made this proposal, and that it has since been revived by a gentleman eminent for his genius, his fine sense and just taste for criticism; but this thought has met with the fate of many useful projects, of being applauded and neglected.

CPSIA information can be obtained at www.ICGtesting.com
Printed in the USA
LVOW120059251111

256390LV00005B/241/A